I CALL HIM
JEHOVAH JIREH
HOW GOD PROVIDED THROUGH THE STORM

Donna S. Goodman

WESTBOW
PRESS®
A DIVISION OF THOMAS NELSON
& ZONDERVAN

WestBow Press books may be ordered through booksellers or by contacting:

WestBow Press
A Division of Thomas Nelson & Zondervan
1663 Liberty Drive
Bloomington, IN 47403
www.westbowpress.com
844-714-3454

ISBN: 978-1-6642-3660-8 (sc)
ISBN: 978-1-6642-3659-2 (e)

Print information available on the last page.

WestBow Press rev. date: 06/16/2021

CONTENTS

Dedication.. vii
Preface.. .ix

CHAPTER 1   "Louisiana Woman, Mississippi Man" 1
CHAPTER 2   "Be Strong and take Courage" 7
CHAPTER 3   "Trust His Heart"......................... 13
CHAPTER 4   Room and Therapy......................... 20
CHAPTER 5   "Packing Up the Dreams God Planted" 26
CHAPTER 6   "His Eye is on the Sparrow" 32
CHAPTER 7   A Stroke of Love.......................... 38
CHAPTER 8   A Place of Healing and Rest.................. 47
CHAPTER 9   Homeward Bound 56
CHAPTER 10   "We Are Witnesses"........................ 65

Bonus Devotions....................................... 71

DEDICATION

*First and foremost, to my husband, Robert who has overcome
so many obstacles to be an inspiration to all who know him.*

*To our sons, Jonathan and Justin, because this stroke didn't just
happen to Robert. It affected the entire family. I could not have
made it through the years without their love, help and encouragement*

*To my dear friends, Maxie and Debbie England, who not only prayed
daily with me while I was employed, but relentlessly encouraged
me to write this book.*

*To our wonderful friends, David and Linda Sobers. God richly
blessed us in 1988 with friends who have been by our side through
thick and thin. Without their love, patience, encouragement,
hope and words of wisdom I couldn't have survived this journey.
Linda reminds me often to take "one day at a time."*

PREFACE

For many years, friends have encouraged me to write a book. Taking care of a stroke survivor and working full time never seemed to offer up the time for such writing. Now, through God's provision, I have the time to tell you my story. "My Story" is really "God's Story" in me. He has been Jehovah Jireh, my provider, in so many ways that are very real and evident, but also in ways that I may never see or realize.

As I prayed over whether I should write this book, I struggled with what kind of book it should be. I had always felt that I should write a devotional book filled with the lessons I've learned through my life's circumstances. Everyday life teaches us so much if we just open our eyes to see. However, so many people expressed a desire to hear about our story that I determined this book should indeed reflect all that God has faithfully done for us through these 25 years following Robert's disabling stroke.

My prayer journal is blank pages with a scripture of gratitude printed on the bottom of every other page. On February 28, 2020, I asked the Lord for clarity concerning this book that you hold in your hand today. When I finished my prayer (I journal my morning prayers as if writing a letter to God), I looked at the scripture printed on the bottom of that page. It read, *"Publish His glorious deeds among the nations. Tell everyone about the amazing things He does." 1 Chronicles 16:24.* Well, that was a really quick and clear answer to my prayer. I have a friend, Diann Greer, who said that she wished God would just write the answer to her prayers on a 3 x 5 card so that she could, without a doubt, know what He wanted her to do. I think I got that card on the bottom of that prayer journal page.

Music has been the center of our lives and service to our Lord. Chapter titles are often the name of a song that may reflect what was happening in our lives at any given moment in time. As God used us to minister to others through praise and worship, it is that very music that has ministered to us through our toughest trials. The people to which we ministered, took the role of ministering to us.

My greatest prayer is that this book will open hearts and lives to see that God provides EVERYTHING that we need. Not just physical provisions and possessions, but peace of heart that comes from accepting His gift of eternal salvation. I desire to spend eternity with you! I know beyond any doubt that eternity will be in heaven. You can have that assurance too.

"LOUISIANA WOMAN, MISSISSIPPI MAN"

CHAPTER 1

Life began for me in that fabulous era called the "fifties". I am a baby boomer. God blessed me abundantly when he gave me wonderful Christian parents whose faith was strong and devotion to each other was unprecedented. They instilled in my two brothers and me a rich heritage of faith in God, strong work ethic and devotion to family. Life was good growing up on a farm in North Louisiana out from a small town called Delhi. Family was all nearby, friends were plenty and we had everything we needed and so much more.

Robert was born and raised in Meridian, MS. He, too, was raised in a Christian home environment with a strong foundation in a local church. He knew that God had called him to the music ministry while still in high school. Preparing for that calling, he attended Mississippi College, a private Baptist college in Clinton, MS, majoring in music. While there, my home church of First Baptist Church, Delhi, LA sought him out to lead worship through music. Since I was already in college at Northeast Louisiana University (now called University of Louisiana at Monroe) I didn't always come home on weekends to attend church. The first time

I met Robert was at a high school football game at the Delhi High School stadium. A mutual friend introduced us. We had a great time and before the evening was over, he stated that he was going to take me home to meet his mother. That was an understatement. Now I had a reason to come home on weekends more often. You could be sure I would be in church alongside my parents every Sunday. During the invitation of a revival service, the Holy Spirit was strongly calling me, setting me apart, to give my life to full time Christian service. I didn't know what, where or how, but I knew His call was for me. I stepped forward to publicly declare God's call in my life.

By this time, Robert had been a regular visitor in our home, particularly for meals. Mom saw this as an opportunity to strengthen a relationship that she would like to see bud. You know the saying, *"The way to a man's heart is through his stomach"*. On one Saturday afternoon in the Fall of 1973, I decided it was time to teach this city boy about the life of a country girl growing up on a farm. It was cotton harvest time, and in those days, the pickers (mechanical, not human) would dump their loads into a large cotton trailer to be carried to the cotton gin for processing. If someone got into the trailer loaded with mounds of cotton and tromped it down, then the trailer would hold more cotton and made for less trips to the gin. We decided this would be a fun and helpful Saturday afternoon activity. There really wasn't much to do in Delhi! As we fell back into the soft cotton, Robert eased over to me to share his heart. He began to explain that he had been praying about whom God would have him to marry. Who would be a mate that would support and encourage him in ministry? He had prayed that prayer on Saturday evening and on Sunday evening, I had come forward to give my life to full time service to our Lord. Robert knew that God was calling me to be his wife.

Since this wasn't exactly a "proposal" neither of us said anything to anyone else. By February of 1974, we were ready to move forward with marriage. Robert asked my dad for permission to marry me and on May 26, 1974, we were married during the Sunday morning worship service at FBC, Delhi. We spent the next year completing our college educations in two different states. We pretty much met on Wednesdays and weekends. In March 1976, God blessed us with a son whose name, Jonathan Robert, means good gift of God. A year later we moved to Water Valley, MS to serve at FBC there. We knew that Robert needed to finish his education by going to seminary. This would be a huge leap of faith to take only the necessities along with our two-year-old child and move to a different state with no job and no place to live. God went before us. He provided every step of the way. By the end of the second day there, we had a place to live and both of us had jobs. God soon led Robert to a part time interim job at North Cleburne Baptist Church in Cleburne, TX and a permanent position at First Baptist Church, Forney, TX. Robert got his Masters in Church Music from Southwestern Baptist Theological Seminary in Ft. Worth, TX in 1980.

Following seminary, we served at First Baptist Church, McComb, MS. It was here that the Lord gave us our second son, Justin Isaac. Just like Sarah laughed when she heard that she would be having a child, I too, laughed because I had so longed for another child. Jonathan was 5 years old and needed a brother. Not only did I laugh to know that I was to have a child, but also Justin has been a source of great laughter in our household. His sense of humor was a joy to experience on so many occasions.

In 1986 God called us to serve at Temple Baptist Church in Hattiesburg, MS. Our tenure there was short but good. The school system was lacking what was needed for our oldest son, so I began to pray about education for both of our boys. God quickly answered that prayer by leading us to Parkview Baptist Church in Baton Rouge, LA. Parkview had an excellent K-12 school that was lacking nothing. As worship leader for the church, the boys attended the school as part of Robert's salary package. After several years there, I was given the privilege of teaching Bible in the school to 7th Graders and Juniors. God had put together a perfect scenario for a family – all of us on the same campus each day.

Life was good! Robert's ministry at the church was growing with a large choir and orchestra for Sunday services and seasonal productions that took the Good News outside the walls of the church to places like the LSU Union Theater and the Baton Rouge Centroplex. The youth choir went on concert tours and mission trips every summer. The adult choir and orchestra presented the musical "God With Us" all over England and Scotland.

While in Baton Rouge we had been blessed with lifelong friends who enriched our lives, enhanced the music ministry and encouraged our hearts. Little did we know how important these dear people would be to us in the days, weeks, months and years that were before us. "A friend loves at all time, and a brother is born for a time of adversity", Proverbs 17:17. There is no greater earthly gift from God than to be blessed with friends.

It is now 1996 and we have been married 22 years. Our oldest son was attending Mississippi College, his dad's alma mater, and Justin was 14 years old having just completed his freshman year of high school. For the first time in our lives, we were preparing to build a house. A house just like we wanted. A house where everything in it is brand new! Robert and I had fixed up so many old houses in our married life that we could have easily had our own HGTV program. Now was the time to start from scratch designing the house that was a perfect fit for us, a family that no longer had small children and would soon be empty nesters. Excitement does not begin to describe our lives. We had purchased the lot in a new growing subdivision surrounding a man-made lake. The plans were drawn, and all was ready to go. We had an open house on Sunday, June 9th and sold our current home that day! It seemed God was lining everything up for the Goodman family to be able to build our dream home.

"God's Plan for You"

God's Word is so full of encouragement to the believer. Yet, to those who do not believe, "those on the outside, may be ever seeing but never perceiving, and ever hearing but never understanding", Mark 4:11-12. When the world looks at Christians, they only see crazy people who are willing to put others first, not striving to be the "top dog" or better than the rest. They can't understand anyone who doesn't desire to wear the highest name brand fashion clothes, live in the finest houses or drive the sportiest cars. To them the Word of God might as well be written only in Greek.

Oh! But for the believer, His word is as clear as a bell and as rich as the finest of crown jewels. My favorite gem from God's word is Jeremiah 29:11, "'For I know the plans I have for you,' declares the Lord, 'plans to prosper you and not to harm you, plans to give you hope and a future.'" God revealed this treasure to me in 1988 and it has since become a priceless promise for me. I do not know where I would be now without His covenant on which to cling.

I can look back and see how God's plan has unfolded for me. I can see how He allowed me to go through struggles to prepare me for what was to come. I know that He taught me and prepared me, in good times as well as bad, for some future event. During this training period, I was totally unaware that I was learning, nor did I have any idea as to how He would use it. God is never finished teaching us or using us for His kingdom's work. "Being confident of this, that He who began a good work in you, will carry it on to completion until the day of Christ Jesus." Philippians 1:6.

You know, it would really be a shame if God invested so much in teaching us and growing us for some specific task and we failed to be the vessels He needed. That is what happens when we don't make ourselves available and sensitive to the leadership of the Holy

Spirit in our lives. When you feel some unexplainable urge to do something kind or out of the ordinary for someone, accept that as God leading you. Be available. Be a vessel. You will be richly blessed.

I want to challenge you to take some time; ask God to reveal specific events in your past that He allowed to happen that prepared you for some later occasion. Write it down. Marvel at how good God has been. I think you will be surprised and pleased at what you see. I love to journal my prayers. It is such an eye-opener to see what God has done and how He has answered our prayers. When we don't write these down, we often forget or don't notice how and when God answered our prayers. God is good, all the time, even when we can't see it. Trust His heart.

Read:
- ➲ Romans 8:28
- ➲ I Thessalonians 5:18
- ➲ Psalm 66:10

"BE STRONG
AND TAKE COURAGE"

──── CHAPTER 2 ────

Thursday, June 13th was a typical summer day for our family. As a school teacher, I was at home with our sons. Robert had gone to work as usual but decided to take the afternoon off to go play golf with 2 men from the choir and orchestra. It was hot, as summers in Baton Rouge typically are. I don't even recall what I did that day, but I imagine it involved staying inside my air-conditioned home.

After playing golf Robert stopped by his office at the church to make sure Ruth, his assistant, didn't need anything else from him concerning the worship service for Sunday. He mentioned to her that he was seeing yellow and black "caution" bars spiraling in his left peripheral vision. At home, he complained of a headache, which was rare for him, but never told me about the vision in his left eye. He ate very little dinner and cleaned up to head to the church for a trustees meeting. When he returned home, his headache had gotten worse. We warmed up one of those things you wrap around your neck for relief and he headed to bed.

At about 2:00 a.m. on Friday morning, June 14th, Robert began to move erratically in the bed. I thought that maybe he was having a bad dream, so I reached over and touched him to wake him and dismiss the dream. He calmed down. I now know that he had not felt me touching him because I was on his left side, which no longer had any feeling in it. In less than a minute he was tossing again. This time, he fell out of the bed. I ran around to see if he had hit his head on the bedside table and to ask if he was okay. When he answered me, his speech was so slurred that I could not even understand his simple, "I'm okay!" I immediately ran to Jonathan's room and shouted, "Call 911! Your dad has had a stroke." Now you need to know that I have not one ounce of medical knowledge in my head. I have to call my friend, Linda, to find out what over the counter pill to take for each different hurt that I have. How I knew it was a stroke was beyond me. After he called 911, I asked him to call Beverly. She was the church organist, but also a nurse in the heart cath unit of Our Lady of the Lake Regional Medical Center. She arrived before the ambulance did and she didn't live close to us!

When the paramedics arrived, they made haste with IV fluids and a quick assessment of the situation. One told me that she thought that his blood sugar had just dropped. I remember telling her that I hoped she was right, but I didn't think she was. I hurriedly got dressed. Jonathan awakened Justin and we prepared for a trip to the Emergency Room. Beverly drove me behind the ambulance and Jonathan drove Justin so that we would have a vehicle at the hospital.

Robert never lost consciousness. He was fully aware of his surroundings. Beverly reminded me that I needed to let our families and the church know what was going on. (Keep in mind, only doctors and rich people had cell phones). Of course, the first person I called was my mom who still lived in Delhi, about a 4-hour drive away. Without hesitation, she said she was on her way! Next, I tried to call his mom, who lived in Gulfport, MS, but she did not answer the phone. In an effort to reach her, I called his sister, Trisha, who lived in Roswell, GA. Her husband Skip answered the phone. Remember this is about three in the morning. He thought that I had identified myself as Dawn, who was their neighbor, so he told me that she was asleep. I'm not sure exactly how I sounded but I told him it was an emergency, could he please wake her up! I needed to let someone from the church know where we were. Robert told me (in his best slurred speech) that I should call Jim Wallace, who was on staff. His reason for contacting Jim was because he was from Six Mile, Alabama and he would be able to understand Robert! Really! Robert was cracking jokes laying in the ER half dead! This was just the beginning of his humor that had heightened in his current state. Some of his other brilliant revelations included: "I guess I'll have to add a stroke to my golf game." "I'll have to increase my handicap in golf." "I can lead music for David Ring." (David Ring is an evangelist who was born with cerebral palsy. His speech is very slurred too.) It was hard not to laugh, but this was certainly no laughing situation. There was little to no medical activity taking place, so we were allowed to be with Robert. I'm not sure why Jonathan had brought "Life's Little Instruction Book" with him, but he did. He began to read some of these instructions to us as we stood around Robert. The ones that we still quote today are, "If you can laugh at it, you can live with it" and "Normal is just a setting on the dryer."

It had been less than a year since we had presented "God With Us" in Great Britain. There was a duet in it entitled, "Be Strong and Take Courage". Jonathan and I had sung that duet. As we waited for what seemed like countless hours in that ER, Jonathan began to sing that song to Robert.

> *"Be strong and take courage,*
> *Do not fear or be dismayed;*
> *For the Lord will go before you,*
> *And His light will show the way.*
> *Be strong and take courage,*
> *Do not fear or be dismayed;*
> *For the One who lives within you*
> *Will be strong in you today.*

Why don't you give Him all of your fears?
Why don't you let Him wipe all of your tears?
He knows! He's been thru pain before,
And He knows all that you've been looking for.

Nothing can take you out of His hand
Nothing can face you that you can't command.
I know that you will always be
In His love; In His power you will be free."

These words ministered as much (or more) to me as they did to Robert. My head was spinning out of control with "what if's". What if he doesn't live? What if he lives, but is permanently an invalid? Where will we live? How will I be able to financially feed and shelter our family? On and on questions were rolling through my head. *"Have I not commanded you? Be strong and courageous. Do not be afraid; do not be discouraged, for the Lord your God will be with you wherever you go." Joshua 1:9* My heart was strengthened by these words of encouragement. I'm so thankful the song writers can put God's Word into song. The combination of music and scripture can calm even the most troubled heart.

"Be Strong and Take Courage" 1985 – Chiasson, Copyright Integrity's Hosanna! Music, Capitol CMG Publishing. All rights reserved, Used by permission

* In writing this, I decided to ask Jonathan why he had that book. This was his response via text since he lives in England now:
"I was just called to it and took it to read while we were in the waiting room for the visitation hours. There were things in there that helped lighten a dark situation (for me) and gave pearls of wisdom to be able to share."

Dr. Pepper

It's my favorite drink – and I get the whole two-liter bottle to myself. Sound familiar? It's a great beverage, but the question always comes up: "Who's going to open the bottle?"

Why is it that this particular drink always fizzes up and spews out the top? Seldom have I seen anyone open it and not get a Dr. Pepper shower. Our oldest son and his best friend came up with an innovative technique: open the bottle slightly, release some pressure, QUICKLY close it back; then finally open it for liquid refreshment. It works!

Have you ever used a quirt bottle of ketchup, only to find it contains mustard? What an unpleasant surprise. Can you imagine what it would be like if you picked up the Crest tube, expecting toothpaste, but you got glue? The contents didn't match the label! This could be very frustrating, and sometimes really embarrassing.

We are all containers, and our labels read, "Christian". However, we are all unique containers: some are Waterford crystal, some Fostoria, some leaded glass and some are just plain peanut butter jars. From time to time, the container gets put under pressure!

When that happens, what comes out? We are told that Christ in us is the hope of glory! What is the first thing out of your mouth under pressure or in a stressful situation? If we're full of Christ, and the good promises in His Word, that should be what comes out. Each day we are faced with many stressful times. How do you react?

If we are filled with Jesus, He's going to be the Light that comes shining forth. When we're under pressure, He can change our shape to endure another hardship, or even enlarge our shape to become a vessel for a new filling. We must first allow ourselves to be filled with Jesus and His Holy Spirit.

We bear Christ's name, but not always His conduct! The story is told of a young soldier under the command of Alexander the Great. During the heat of battle, the young many deserted the troops. He was caught and brought before the military commander. The commander asked the young soldier his name. When he replied, "Alexander, sir", the great general said, "Son, either change your ways or change your name!" We must show the character and nature of Christ in all we do. He is the hope of glory in us!

What's your attitude like under pressure? What's the first thing out of your mouth in a dilemma or when you hit the wrong nail with the hammer? Today make the commitment to respond – not react – to pressure.

Read:
➲ Colossians 1:27
➲ II Corinthians 4:7
➲ James 1:12
➲ Matthew 5:14-16

(This devotion was written by Robert in June 1991 for a youth choir tour.)

"TRUST HIS HEART"

— CHAPTER 3 —

As the sun began to rise outside the walls of this enormous hospital, I was reminded that this was the day that our Lord had made. I wasn't so sure about being able to rejoice and be glad in it. Let's be honest and not judgmental here; I really couldn't see any reason to rejoice. Haven't you had days like that?

Robert was moved to SICU (Surgical Intensive Care Unit) even though there had been no surgery involved. We were led to the family waiting room to sit and wait and pray. It wasn't long before the room began to fill up with church members who were our friends, our family away from home, our encouragement, God in flesh that offered hope and peace. More than once, these people joined hands to form a huge circle of prayer warriors. Since this was a Friday, many had to go to work. One by one, the number of supporters slowly decreased, but rarely were we ever alone in that waiting room. Since Beverly worked at the same hospital, she would stop by in between procedures to check on us. The phone on the waiting room desk was constantly ringing with inquiries as to his condition from friends who were too far away to come. Facebook didn't exist! I recall how humbled and blessed I was when Don and Stella, our friends from Forney, TX traveled all the way to Baton Rouge to be with me and to see Robert. I had a sweet well-meaning friend quietly slip me some of her tranquilizer pills. Whispering softly, she said I would need one. I couldn't wait to get to the restroom and flush those down the toilet. I knew that my God could and would handle whatever I had to face in the days ahead.

Later in the day, the Social Services nurse escorted the boys and me to a small room to discuss his condition and what we could anticipate in the days ahead. She explained that the right frontal lobe of his brain had been deprived of blood and was basically dead. That particular lobe was the center for such things as creativity, self-discipline and self-control, short term memory, logic, as well as, the control of muscles on the left side of his body. She told us that there was a chance that he had lost all of his ability to read music because that was considered creative. When she said that he would be very self-oriented or selfish, I almost rebuked her. I remember telling her that she could not possibly be talking about the man to whom I was married.

He had selflessly given his entire life to serving others. He never hesitated to leave the warmth and comfort of his bed in the wee hours of the morning to go to the hospital to encourage and pray with anyone who called on him. We had served as decoys in an airport to rescue a sweet friend from an abusive situation. When an engine that a choir member was working on blew up and severely burned him, Robert got to the hospital before the ambulance did. Another choir member's husband working on an oil rig was covered with acid and jumped into the muddy Mississippi River to wash off the poison. In so doing, he also exposed his damaged skin to all the germs that the mighty Mississippi water held. Robert was there in a heartbeat. He was selfless in his love and devotion to his family as well. He never spent the money he received from the choir at Christmas on himself. It was always spent on the boys and me. I could go on and on of his faithfulness to be the hands and feet of God. How could this man be selfish?

There were so many hours of waiting in that room for the short window of time that we could go into his ICU room for a few minutes and be with him. When the time came, every visit was like being on a roller coaster. Some visits gave us hope that he was doing good. Other visits broke my heart because he didn't respond at all. There were tubes in every part of his body. He did manage to pull one out that he didn't like. He was medicated to relieve the pain in his head. When they fed him through the feeding tube, his heart stopped. He recalled the nurse running into his room, jumping on the bed, straddling him and proceeding with CPR. Shortly afterwards they inserted a temporary pacemaker. His heart stopped two more times after that, but the pacemaker kicked in to keep him alive. Unfortunately, Robert's mother and Justin were in his room on one of the occasions that his heart stopped. Even with the pacemaker, it was a traumatic experience. This really disturbed them both to witness the brevity of life. It was still very uncertain as to whether or not he would live.

Robert had always been the primary bread winner in our family and had always managed the finances in our home. It wasn't that I did not have the skills to do so, but that he felt it was his responsibility as the head of the household. I had studied some accounting in college and had worked for several CPAs in my life. I knew how, but he chose to take that responsibility. As a minister, Robert was considered self-employed. I'm not sure exactly when it hit me that June 15th was the day that another self-employment tax payment was due. June 15th was a Saturday which meant, it was technically not due to be mailed until, Monday, June 17th. I was frantic. I didn't know where the forms were, how much to pay, where to find the funds that he had stashed somewhere. Panic almost overcame me. Dealing with the government has never been tops on my list of fun things to do and I sure didn't want to get on their bad side. God provides. Before teaching, I had worked for a CPA who was a member of our church orchestra. I called Paul and he calmed me down and helped me through every step of the process, reassuring me all the way.

Sunday, June 16th was Father's Day! The ICU nurses were a little more lenient with the two-visitor limit and allowed all three of us (Jonathan, Justin and me) into his room at one time to celebrate his day! He was still in and out of awareness due to medication. He also remained in much pain due to the swelling of the brain. We helped him use his one functioning hand to tear away the wrappings from his gift. This was a terribly painful thing for me to watch. More than once I had to turn away and cry. My heart questioned over and over again, how could this be the 43-year-old father of my sons? How could this man with LOW blood pressure who exercised every day be lying here almost dead from a stroke?

After removing the feeding tube, the medical team began to test his ability to swallow. The one thing that Robert hated the most was an item called "Thick It". This was put in ALL food items that had any form of liquid matter, including water. They cautiously fed him water to see if he would swallow it or aspirate on it. Getting anything in his lungs would have been catastrophic to his recovery.

As worship leader, Robert had prepared the choir and orchestra to present a beautiful song entitled *"Trust His Heart"* by Babbie Mason. The words of this song played over and over in my head. I found such comfort in knowing that no matter what, I could trust my God to see me through whatever was before me. The staff at Parkview found someone to lead worship in Robert's absence that Sunday. It was with eyes filled with tears and hearts broken by their love for this dear man that they attempted to sing these words:

All things work for our good
Though sometimes we don't see how they could
Struggles that break our hearts in two
Sometimes blind us to the truth
Our Father knows what's best for us
His ways are not our own
So when your pathway grows dim
And you just don't see Him,
Remember you're never alone

God is too wise to be mistaken
God is too good to be unkind
So when you don't understand
When don't see His plan
When you can't trace His hand
Trust His Heart

He sees the master plan
He holds our future in His hand,
So don't live as those who have no hope,
All our hope is found in Him
We see the present clearly
But He sees the first and the last
And like a tapestry He's weaving you and me,
To someday be just like Him

God's Presence in Our Lives

A sign hangs above my desk that reads: "Dear God, so far today, I've done all right. I haven't gossiped or lost my temper. I haven't been greedy or selfish or overindulgent. I've been living in your will and concentrating on what I can do for others. But God, in a few minutes, I'm going to get out of bed and from then on, I'm probably going to need a lot more help! Amen." Isn't it true? We should stop each morning before we get out of bed just to realize how desperately we need God. If we would, I'm sure there would be a lot more of us having a quiet time with God each morning.

This started me to think of just a few of the things that God provides for us as we face each day. I explored God's word to find the scriptures that remind us of the help we can find in His promises.

STRENGTH: Philippians 4:13 says, "I can do everything through Him who gives me strength." One of Webster's definitions for strength is "ability of the mind". Isn't it nice to know that our Lord can give us not only muscular strength to face a physically fatiguing day, but also strength of the mind? (I think that might be called "attitude".)

COMFORT: II Corinthians 1:3-4 states, "Praise be to the God and Father of our Lord Jesus Christ, the Father of compassion and the God of all comfort, who comforts us in all our troubles," but it doesn't end there. God has a reason for giving us this comfort. Read on, "so that we can comfort those in any trouble with the comfort we ourselves have received from God." (A gift with a purpose)

PEACE: In I Corinthians 14:33, Paul is addressing a problem in the church of disorderly worship because everyone is trying to prophecy at the same time. Nevertheless, what he states applies to our daily lives. "For God is not a God of disorder but of peace." Jesus is the Prince of Peace. When I think of the peace that God gives, I immediately envision a white dove gently cooing his song of peace. (Rest a minute in that peace.)

GUIDANCE: Psalm 23:3, "He guides me in paths of righteousness for His name's sake." Would you leave home today to drive to North Church, New Jersey (a small town randomly selected) without a map or GPS? I wouldn't. Yet, many of us try to get through the day without our guide, the guide God has waiting for us.

HOPE: Colossians 1:27, "To them God has chosen to make known among the Gentiles the glorious riches of this mystery, which is Christ in you, the hope of glory." (that needs no further comment)

PLAN: Jeremiah 29:11, "'For I know the plans I have for you,' declares the Lord, 'plans to prosper you and not to harm you, plans to give you hope and a future.'" Did you take the time to find out God's plan for your day, or did you set out to follow your own plans? I can assure you; His plan is better.

To this list I must add Galatians 5:22, "But the fruit of the spirit if love, joy, peace, patience, kindness, goodness, faithfulness, gentleness and self-control." God offers us so much, but we often refuse to take it.

Please take the time each day to receive all that God offers you. He truly desires to bless us far beyond what we could ever dream. Allow Him to truly be "Lord" of your life today.

ROOM AND THERAPY

After 6 days in ICU, he was transferred to the telemetry floor for observation since his heart had stopped and the temporary pacemaker had been inserted. I don't recall when the pacemaker was removed, but once the feeding tube was removed, the heart problem seemed to go away. The medical team was cautious and wanted to be prepared in case his heart stopped again.

He was only on the telemetry floor for a couple of days before he was moved to a regular room. Being like an overprotective mother, I did not want him to be left alone so I spent most of my days and every night in his room.

His mental handicaps began to show up now that he was able to converse, though the speech was still slurred. He insisted that we needed to get the groceries that he had purchased at Sam's Club out of the trunk of the car. In his mind, he had gone to Sam's and bought items for the church. He was supposed to do that on Friday the 14th, but obviously that didn't happen. In his mind, he had gone. I could not convince him that there were no groceries in the car. Finally, I told him we took them out, just to let that issue go.

Because of the medications for pain, he was having hallucinations. Our Lady of the Lake Regional Medical Center is a Catholic hospital. Every room has a crucifix hanging over the head of the bed. The TV is mounted on the opposite wall at the foot of the bed. When the TV was off, the patient could see the reflection of the crucifix in the black screen. Robert saw that crucifix, but Jesus became like Elvis and jumped off the cross, playing a guitar in true Elvis form. Yikes! "If you can laugh at it, you can live with it!" His lack of self-control also began to be evident. Our sweet friend, Anna, stopped by Baskin Robbins and picked up a quart of his favorite ice cream. He kept eating and eating until I thought he surely would explode. I encouraged him to save some for later. The nursing staff would put it in their freezer for him. Nope. Wouldn't have it. He ate the entire quart!

All was not gloomy and sad in Robert's world. His sense of humor really lightened the circumstances. On one visit to his room in ICU, he asked for the remote control for the TV. This was a definite sign that he was feeling better. After giving it to him, I noticed that he began to change the channels without even opening his eyes to see what was on. When I asked him why he was doing that, his response was, "to aggravate you." Yep, he was on the road to healing! While Don and Stella went in to visit, he kept them entertained with statements like, "When you lay around all day without your clothes on, you can get a lot of things done." "If my red light (oxygen monitor on his finger) were blue, I could have a blue light special." Jonathan told his dad, "the MRI says you still have a brain", to which Robert responded with, "Well you don't, according to the university!"

Once he became stable, it was time to start physical, occupational and speech therapy. Because he had been flat on his back in the bed for so long, sitting up made him nauseated. The first day was very stressful for him. I was told that physical therapy dealt with the lower extremities of his body such as walking, standing, sitting. Occupational therapy dealt with his upper extremities like picking up cones, wiggling fingers and all those little things that we take for granted in our daily lives. Speech therapy not only taught him how to talk without slurring his words, but also memory, logic and other cognitive skills. So much had changed in his brain. His physical condition was only a small part of the damage the stroke had done. It was explained to me that to Robert's brain, the left side of his body did not exist. If you drew a line from head to toe down the center of your body and removed the left side of your body, then your center axis would be in the center of the right side of your body – all that exists in your brain. This causes your balance to focus on only the right side and thus likely to tip over because your weight was unevenly distributed. Vision was a similar situation. His left eye had total sight, but his brain could not process what it was seeing. This was called left neglect. If you placed your left hand, palm to the right, vertical from your forehead to the tip of your nose, then closed your left eye, that is what Robert's brain processes for sight. He had to learn to completely turn his head to the left to see what was on that side of his body. Even today, 24 years later, if you approach him from his left side, he does not comprehend that you are there.

His left vocal cords were paralyzed as well. During times of rest he would put headphones on and sing along with music that he so dearly loved. My heart ached as I listened to this man with a master's degree in music with emphasis in vocal performance, not be able to match pitch or sustain a note. I remember asking God how in the world we were going to financially survive. His entire career had been based on his ability to sing.

There was a constant flow of loving people who stopped by to see Robert and me. Members of our church and choir, other ministers in the area, people who had been in previous churches in which we had served came from other states, former staff members who had served as Robert's music associates, and the list goes on. Gifts, flowers, balloons, food came in abundance. Little children would crawl up in his hospital bed and give warm hugs and expressions of love. I was overwhelmed and comforted by such an outpouring of concern for us as a family. Couples would come by and while the husband stayed with Robert, the wife would take me across the street to get a hot healthy meal and just let me talk! What a blessing a small thing is! Other families would be sure that our sons were fed and engaged in wholesome activities in the community of believers.

When July 4th rolled around, I asked permission to take Robert outside the building to the lawn of the hospital for a picnic. I prepared a typical Independence Day outdoor meal with a special surprise for Robert. I brought his beloved dog, Chaps, to the picnic. There was such a joyous reunion of the two. I'm not sure which one was happiest to see the other. I spread a blanket on the lawn, Janell brought his favorite chocolate pie and we dined as if we were celebrating on the banks of our favorite lake! Robert, of course, remained in his wheelchair the entire time. It was very hot and he was weak and tired very easily. Time was short, but the memory remains sweet. It was a July 4th celebration like no other. Healing comes in so many ways. A picnic on the outside of a hospital building can do more to heal the spirit than a lot of therapy can do inside the walls of an institution. Later that evening, after he rested, I took him to the top floor of the hospital where we watched the fireworks over the Mississippi River that was a Baton Rouge tradition. It was a good day!

God Paints the Sunrise

When I was ten years old, my baby brother Bob was born. I recall sitting outside in the early evening hours of the summer on the swing watching the beautiful sunsets. Mom always told baby Bob and me that God had painted that sunset as a gift for each of us. The sunsets that God paints are, at best, pretty compared to the sunrises I've experienced recently. When I experience a sunrise, I remind myself that God painted that just for me. They are not only breathtaking in visual beauty, but a message for my heart from Him as well.

Sunrises are always so far away, (and some would say, "so early!") It is much too distant for us to reach out and touch. It may look like velvet, but we will never know because our sense of touch can never be filled with a sunrise. If we could get close to a sunrise, our finite vision could only see the portion that was directly in front of us, thus eliminating the overall beauty of the big picture that makes it so magnificent. We have to think about the fact that people thousands of miles away can see and experience that same sunrise because it is so far reaching.

Quite frequently, there is something in the way to obscure the total vision of the sunrise. It may be trees, buildings, mountains, power lines or a host of other objects. How enchanting a sunrise could be if there was no obstruction.

In addition to obstructions, change is a factor in a sunrise. Have you ever noticed how rapidly a sunrise changes? The colors are constantly evolving as the sun pops up from the horizon. How wonderful it would be if we could just stop time and absorb each color change before it moves on to the next.

Life is like that! The beauty always seems to be just out of our reach. We always think that better days are out there in the future, but not right her, right now. However, when we get too close, we can't see the big picture. The beauty in the entire masterpiece of our life is blurred because we are too focused on the here and now. God paints our lives with as much attention to detail as he does each sunrise – unique and special. That is what makes life beautiful.

The objects that obscure our view are the trials and struggles of life that Satan wants to use to cover the real beauty of our life in Christ. We must look beyond those "trees" to see the captivating, breath-taking blessings of life. Like a sunrise, our single, solitary life touches the entire earth by touching the lives of others on a daily basis.

We would love to hold on to those beautiful moments in time (like wedding, birth of a child, celebration of salvation, etc.) and treasure that feeling forever. However, the exuberance fades as routine life returns, but we can cherish the memories forever. As the beauty of the rich sunrise is replaced by the brightness of full sun on another day, we must step boldly and brightly into our lives embracing the hope and promise that it brings.

Oh, to capture a sunrise with paint instead of words. I am thankful that God can paint inspiration in my heart as beautiful as one of His sunrises!

Read:
➲ Psalm 27:4
➲ I Peter 3:4

"PACKING UP THE DREAMS GOD PLANTED"

CHAPTER 5

As you recall, we had sold our house on Sunday, before Robert suffered his stroke on Friday. We had to move! Where? For the first time in my life, I thought about Jesus as the "homeless" person that He was. I had no clue how we would live; where we would live; what to do with all our possessions! My brain was on overload. My goodness, we still had sons at "home" that were dependent on us as parents! How could this be happening to our happy, normal family? Fact of the matter was, we had to get all this stuff out of this house.

While Robert was in therapy during the day, I would go to the house and pack. Jonathan and Justin were so very helpful. On one such day, we were very busy packing when the guidance counsellor from Parkview Baptist School, Bill Dawson, called. He said that he hated to ask me this, but they were wondering if I would teach the Senior Bible class in the upcoming year of school instead of the Junior Class. What you need to understand is that there was no written curriculum for these Bible classes. I had developed the lesson plan for teaching Acts to the Juniors and after 4 years of teaching it, I felt very comfortable with the instruction. To start from scratch with a new curriculum would be extremely time consuming outside the classroom. With my life in total disarray, I couldn't imagine giving endless hours to developing a new plan. I begged Bill to not do this to me. He listened quietly and said that he would see what he could do. I hung up the phone, fell face down on the floor and sobbed, mourning much like I imagine the Hebrews doing on many occasions in the Bible. Jonathan and Justin came running in there to see what in the world was going on. I think they must have thought that Robert had died! They stood there looking at me, not knowing what to do to console me. After a moment, I stood up, wiped my eyes and proceeded to give them instructions about continuing to pack. I had my first melt down. By the way, I taught the Junior class the following year.

Jehovah Jireh, my provider, really made evident His abundant provision through this time in my life. Since we had no house in which to put our possessions, a precious friend, Harvine, located a climate-controlled facility for us. She and her husband, Guy, took care of all the arrangements and fees. God provided. The deacons of the church made arrangements for a moving company to take all our worldly goods to the storage facility. They also paid for this service. God provided. This was all good, but we couldn't live in the storage facility! Vera, a widow with a large house, opened her heart and home to us. We moved in with her. God provided. Determined to move ahead with our plans to build, we needed to tweak our plans in case total handicap accessibility was needed. Our friend and architect, Glen, came to the hospital to help me iron out those changes to the plans. No charge. God provided. It didn't take long for a widow who had only raised one child, a daughter, to get her fill of teenage boys. Though she would have tolerated us much longer, I felt that for the sanity of everyone involved, we needed to get out on our own. A church member who dealt in real estate, "rented" us an apartment for $1. God provided. Our furniture was in storage and had not been put in there so that we could readily access beds and chairs. Church members came to the rescue with provisions that would never be featured in *"House Beautiful"* but certainly met our needs. This was probably the only time that we lived with cardboard boxes as bedside tables. It is amazing what you can live without! God provided.

As soon as Robert was released from the hospital (oh happy day!), it was time for me to return to teaching. My entire summertime off had been consumed with stroke and moving. Even though he was released from the hospital, he still had to go to therapy appointments every day. While Justin and I were at school and Jonathan was at LSU, church members took turns taking Robert to therapy. Many times, they would treat him to lunch. God provided. Casseroles were brought to the apartment often by friends who were pretty sure that I didn't have time to cook. God provided.

This first year was a very difficult one. Our lives had been completely turned upside down. Our friend, Pat, paid for us, as a family to receive counselling to learn to adjust to this new "normal". Remember, normal is just a setting on the dryer. God provided.

Robert could no longer work, yet the church continued to pay his salary for that entire year. God provided. As a young minister, Robert had taken out disability insurance. His father had health issues, so Robert wanted to be sure that his family would be taken care of in case he too suffered from failing health. Many times, as a young couple struggling to pay bills, I asked Robert if that disability insurance was necessary. In Robert's wisdom, he never dropped it. God provided. Also, when one is ordained to the ministry, the government gives them the option of paying into Social Security or not. Robert had opted to pay, therefore providing Social Security disability in addition to his private insurance. God provided. Getting the Social Security disability was a struggle. After being denied for the third time, we secured an attorney in the church and had a hearing to determine that his disability was legitimate. It was so difficult to sit before those judges who held the outcome for our future in their hands and admit to the handicaps and challenges that my husband faced each day. I drew my strength from the Lord knowing that He was the One Who held our future in His hands and that these men had only the power that God had given them. God provided. Receiving Social Security Disability also provided for Robert, medical insurance through Medicare. This alone was a tremendous blessing, knowing that his future would be heavy laden with medical expenses. God provided.

Though we had good medical insurance through my employment as a teacher, it did have limits on how much therapy it would pay. For a time, it paid for physical and occupational therapy, but speech was considered an unnecessary function and therefore did not pay for speech therapy. Pat who had already paid for counselling was a speech therapist. She provided months of therapy for him, in our apartment at no charge. God provided. Every fall Parkview Baptist School hosted a very large craft fair as a fundraiser for the school. Vera (with whom we had lived) organized this event. The choir members of PVBC secured a sweet shop booth to raise funds for Robert's continued therapy. Every person made and donated items to sell with 100% of the proceeds going to private pay for occupational and physical therapy. Becky Thomas' fudge was the "hot" item that brought in lots of money. In order to make as much as possible, money was donated to purchase ingredients for fudge. Sugar was purchased in 25-pound bags; marshmallow cream by the case; chocolate chips in huge quantities. About 10 friends came to Becky and Barry's house, stood around their island cooktop and stirred four batches on four burners at a time. When one got done, we washed the saucepan and started over. For hours, we were a fudge making factory. This was a bonding time for all involved as much fun and laughter rang out while serving others. In all, the choir raised over $6,000 to further Robert's therapy! Unheard of! God provided.

"So Abraham called that place The Lord Will Provide. And to this day it is said, "On the mountain of the Lord, it will be provided." Genesis 22:14. Jehovah Jireh is the name that is given to the Lord, my God Who is and always will be my provider. I have learned to trust in the provision that God has for me. He has never failed me and He never will.

"Healthy, Wealthy & Wise"

American Southern tradition says that in order to be healthy, wealthy and wise in the upcoming new year, we must consume certain foods for our New Year's Day meal. Black-eyed peas, cabbage, pork and cornbread have been a staple on my menu for my entire life that I can recall. I did a little research and found that the peas symbolize coins or wealth; greens (cabbage or turnip) resemble money, specifically folding money; pork is considered a sign of prosperity because pigs root forward; cornbread symbolizes gold because corn kernels represent coins. So far, I am not a millionaire by the world's standards. I do, however, have a storehouse full of wealth when it comes to friends.

When Jonathan was a small child of four or five, we went to visit my grandmother in her small, modest home in my hometown. Upon entering her den and viewing several shelves on the wall filled with family photos, Jonathan was overwhelmed and exclaimed, "Oh, she must be very rich!" How true: There was so much wisdom in that statement made by a young innocent child. Grandmother was indeed rich in love of her family. I have cherished that moment and recall it often when I find my focus has turned worldly.

Traditionally, we watch "It's A Wonderful Life" every year during the holiday season. I must have seen this movie fifty times in my life, yet I never grow tired of the message it teaches. This year, I heard a statement that had slipped past me during those other forty-nine times I had seen it. The inscription in the book left by Clarence for George Bailey said, "Remember, no man is a failure who has friends." Not only are we not a failure if we have friends, but we are also rich.

When trials and struggles, large or small come our way, it is so comforting to know that we have a wealth of friends on whom we can depend. But even more comforting is the fact that "there is a friend who sticks closer than a brother." Proverbs 18:24. Jesus is that friend. He also tells us in John 15:13-14, "Greater love has no one than this, that he lay down his life for his friends. You are my friends if you do what I command." Isn't it wonderful to know that Jesus is such a great friend that He would not only offer to lay down His life for us, His friends, He did it. My prayer for you and myself would be that we draw closer to that friend than we have ever been. In order to grow closer to someone, you must first know them and accept them as your friend. If you don't know Jesus as your friend and Savior, please search your heart and find Him today. He is a friend worth finding.

"HIS EYE IS ON THE SPARROW"

⸺ CHAPTER 6 ⸺

After months of only going to church on Sunday mornings, I felt it was time for me to try to attend choir rehearsal and get back to singing praises to God in choir in Sunday worship. Practice for choir was on Wednesday nights. I could say, "For some unknown reason" I entered the church through the front glass doors instead of the usual side doors which were closer to the choir room. Now I know it was for a very good reason that I chose a different door. God had a very special message for me.

The sun had not yet set, and a beautiful dusk sky painted my world with color that settled into my heart like peace. After soaking in God's artistry, I had just entered the doors when I heard a thud on the glass behind me. I turned to see that a lovely female cardinal had flown into the glass and fallen to the pavement below. A blue jay that had been chasing her quickly landed and began to torment her. Not on my watch! That blue jay had done enough damage. I opened the door and stepped out to shoo the enemy away from the fallen cardinal.

She looked so pitiful laying there on her back. She was blinking her eyes and her breath was panting so I knew she was still alive.

Though full of fear both from the blue jay and from this large human creature standing over her, she could not move. My heart was broken for her. I knelt down beside her and began to stroke her beautiful chest. I'm sure that wasn't calming to her, but it made me feel better. Immediately, the words to that beautiful old hymn, *"His Eye is on the Sparrow"* came to mind. I began to softly sing that song to the bird, tears streaming down my face.

"Why should I feel discouraged?
Why should the shadows come?
Why should my heart be lonely
and long for heaven and home,
when Jesus is my portion?
My constant friend is He:
His eye is on the sparrow,
and I know He watches me;
His eye is on the sparrow,
and I know He watches me.
'Let not your heart be troubled,'
his tender word I hear,
and resting on His goodness,
I lose my doubts and fears;
though by the path He leadeth
but one step I may see:
His eye is on the sparrow,
and I know he watches me;
his eye is on the sparrow,
and I know He watches me.
Whenever I am tempted,
whenever clouds arise,
when song gives place to sighing,
when hope within me dies,
I draw the closer to Him;
from care He sets me free:

His eye is on the sparrow,
and I know He watches me;
His eye is on the sparrow,
and I know He watches me.
Refrain:
I sing because I'm happy,
I sing because I'm free,
for His eye is on the sparrow,
and I know He watches me."

Public Domain

David Sobers, the church's sound technician, who had been upstairs in the sound booth, right above where this scene was happening, came down to see if everything was okay. He quickly saw that I was having a moment with God and returned to his project.

I don't know how long I sat there by that precious creation of God's, but it was long enough to witness her recover and fly away. At that moment there was nothing more beautiful to me than her flight back to life. Life as a cardinal. Life as a mother bird. A life filled with the song that God had created her to sing.

This event wasn't just a coincidental happening. The timing, the front door of the church (which I NEVER used), the cardinal, the blue jay, David were all carefully planned and carried out by my divine heavenly Father. He had a very important message for me played out just like Jesus had used stories to illustrate His message to the people in Biblical days.

I was beginning to get the picture. My life was represented by this little female cardinal. Life was beautiful as I flew along being a wife, mother, teacher, minister's wife, friend and much more. Without warning, Satan chased after me with such fervor, that I ran smack into that glass wall. My world was turned upside down. I could only lie there flat on my back, panting and full of fear for the future. I had gone from being the supportive help mate alongside my husband to being the dominant responsible person who was now taking care of a very dependent, insecure man that I barely recognized. All financial decisions, spiritual leadership in the home, and parenting responsibilities fell on me. I wasn't prepared. When David came down to check on me, I knew that God had given me His hands and feet wrapped in human flesh. Friends that would always be there to help me through this crisis of life. So many times, I wondered how anyone could get through these kinds of life events without God and the fellowship of believers that would be there to support and encourage them. The answer is, they can't.

That evening God clearly communicated to me that He would never leave me. He had created me with a song to sing and it was time to soar on wings of eagles and proclaim His message through music. It has been almost 25 years at the time of this writing since that precious cardinal and I had our encounter, but it remains fresh in my heart and mind as if it were yesterday. I can hear all kinds of birds singing outside my window as I write, but the song of the cardinal rings loudest in my ear. As Henry van Dyke stated: "Use what talents you possess; The woods would be very silent if no birds sang there except those that sang best."

"Are not two sparrows sold for a penny? Yet not one of them will fall to the ground outside your Father's care. And even the very hairs of your head are all numbered. So don't be afraid; you are worth more than many sparrows." Matthew 10:29-31. In this case, I knew this little cardinal was representing the sparrow in God's Word and that God would take care of me because I am worth so much more that any sparrow or cardinal to Him. In that moment, Jehovah Shalom, the God of Peace became very evident to me. My favorite scripture is found in Jeremiah 29:11 and states, "'For I know the plans I have for you,' declares the Lord, 'plans to prosper you and not to harm you, plans to give you hope and a future.'" This, my friend, is a promise in which I find my security and hope. You can too!

"Sewing Joy"

A very special gift from God to me is the gift of creativity. One of the greatest pleasures I have is creating by using my sewing machine. I am blessed by God as one of the few people left in "modern" America who actually enjoys sewing. God has opened my eyes to look at my sewing machine from a different perspective, a spiritual perspective.

The first thing I must do before any sewing can be done is turn on the power switch. Likewise, the Holy Spirit must stir in our hearts and convict us of our need for salvation, but He doesn't leave us there powerless to do anything about it. God is our source of power! He wants to empower us with His love, salvation, strength, peace and the list goes on. We are nothing without the power of God's presence in our lives, just like my sewing machine is useless without electricity.

Once I have power, then I need thread. I see thread as our salvation because without it, all the other parts of the machine are useless. It is our salvation that ties all the rest of our life together. Lives have no continuity when Christ is not the head of them. We would flounder around aimlessly without that thread that binds our hearts and lives to God.

When the thread is pulled from the spool, it is guided by several hooks and eyes to point it in the proper direction. This series of thread guides is like the Word of God. The Bible is full of directional instruction to help us find God's will for our lives. It is pretty useless though if we don't read it and obey it. God has a customized plan for your life, but we must be willing to submit to the guide to find the right way.

I've noticed that one very necessary part of my machine is a little item called the tension dial. You see, the thread must pass through this dial in order to have a set amount of pressure placed on it. This keeps the thread from running away, leaving big loops and ugly stitches that don't serve the purpose of holding the fabric pieces together. Our lives are like that. Without the everyday stresses and the gigantic crisis in our lives, we would never learn to trust God. We would run ahead of God and leave big loops and ugly actions in our path, not serving the purpose that God has for us. Without trials, we would tend to feel pretty confident in ourselves and not in God.

There is another dial that is controlled by me. It is called the stitch length regulator. This obviously determines the length of each stitch. How far do you reach out with the Word of God? To the people at work, to friends, to strangers? You control this. Is your stitch length long enough?

One of the final destinations for the thread is through the eye of the needle. This small hole at the end of the sharp needle is where the thread finally meets the fabric. The sharp piercing action of the needle penetrates the textile, leaving behind the thread. Remember, at the beginning of this writing, the thread was salvation, now the fabric represents the life of the unbeliever who needs to know Christ. Just like the pressure foot guides the fabric into the path of the needle, so the Holy Spirit guides the lives of people into our path for the purpose of meeting with God's Word. God puts them there so His Word can penetrate their hearts.

After the thread penetrates the textile, it reaches down below to the bobbin, which is also filled with thread. I like to think of the bobbin as other believers and the entwining of the two as fellowship with believers. This makes the stitch complete, just like friendship with Christians makes our lives complete.

Every part of the machine, thread, fabric, and bobbin are necessary parts in order to be able to successfully create a garment, a quilt, or anything else artistic using needle and thread. When we have followed the guides, gone through the tension and penetrated the fabric to fellowship with others, we find a beautiful creation of joy that only God can make.

A STROKE OF LOVE

— CHAPTER 7 —

As I previously mentioned, the first year was a very difficult one. Aside from the counselling that our friend had given us as a family, Our Lady of the Lake Regional Medical center had a counsellor on staff that was provided for stroke survivors and caregivers. These people were all very wise, educated and understanding people, but they lacked one thing: they had not lived the life we were facing each day. Their knowledge and advice came from a book. There was no relationship to what we were living. I longed to connect with people who knew firsthand exactly what surviving this catastrophic illness was like.

One year after the stroke, it was time for us to break away from financial dependence on Parkview Baptist Church and school. After prayer and council from Godly friends and advisors, we delved into the realm of a non-profit organization that would unite stroke survivors and their families who lived in or near Baton Rouge. A Stroke of Love Ministries was born. Getting all the legal paperwork completed and approved by the government of Louisiana is no small task. God provided an attorney who was there every step of the way giving us advice and help at no charge.

On June 6, 1997, Parkview Baptist Church hosted a banquet to launch this new ministry. The entire church turned out to not only wish us well, but to show their financial support for A Stroke of Love. Robert was given the opportunity to direct the choir one last time singing his favorite song, "The Majesty and Glory of Your Name". Both of us spoke to the congregation that we so dearly loved, sharing with them our hopes and dreams for this new ministry. Our desire was to have regular monthly stroke survivor support group meetings. Our Lady of the Lake graciously allowed us to use a meeting room in their facilities at no charge. Some months we would have a guest speaker, and sometimes it was just survivors and caregivers sharing their hearts, struggles, and resources that had been helpful to them.

In order to help fund this ministry (aside from monthly contributions from dear friends), we traveled to churches and other organizations speaking and singing. Robert's vocal cords on the left side were now paralyzed, so singing was not of the same caliber it had been. Though his emphasis in college had been vocal performance and with all the speech therapy he had received, his ability to sing had not returned. He did, however, "make a joyful noise unto God". His part in our presentation was speaking. Often times, he had to really concentrate on articulating his words. Also, with short term memory loss, it was very difficult for him to recall what he had just said. We arrived equipped with a notebook clearly laid out and highlighted to help us stay on track. There were so many churches that received us very openly and always someone who needed to hear God's message through us. The theme of our message was to not waste our struggles. All of us are or have been or will be going through difficulty. Don't waste it. Learn from it. Stroke survivors, caregivers, cancer patients, people who have lost their jobs, on and on the list goes. We all have a lesson to learn.

To lighten the subject, Robert could always find humor in the situation. One of his favorite sayings was "I can hide my own Easter eggs" in reference to his short-term memory loss.

God opened the door to several opportunities for us to publicly proclaim His faithfulness through media. Robert was interviewed for a local morning news human interest story on WBRZ television station in Baton Rouge, LA. Our friend and news anchor Leo Honeycutt authored this news story. When Leo asked Robert if he ever asked God, "Why me?", Robert was quick to respond with "Why not me?" Why should any of us be immune to trials and struggles. The verse that we chose to be our "theme" for A Stroke of Love was James 1:2-3, "Consider it pure joy, my brothers and sisters whenever you face trials of many kinds, because you know that the testing of your faith produces perseverance." Robert had been on the morning show many times during his years as Minister of Music at PVBC promoting various programs that were open to the public, so he was a very recognized individual in the city. This story, however, was totally different from his previous interviews. His appearance publicized the stroke support group in the area, getting word out to many who were unchurched or had not yet heard of the meetings.

The Advocate, which was the Baton Rouge newspaper, did a full-page article about us which was on the cover of the religious section, complete with color photo. Again, the word of our faith through this trial was in the hands of the public.

Kathy Chapman-Sharp was a writer for many Lifeway publications. Lifeway is the largest publisher of literature and magazines for the Southern Baptist Convention. Each month, several magazines are published for distribution to churches both in the United States and abroad. Kathy and her husband Terry had previously served on staff with us at First Baptist Church, McComb, MS. When she heard of our story, she got permission to write an article about our testimony for an issue of Home Life. This magazine targeted adults of all ages, providing stories of news interest and human interest from a Christian perspective. Again, God was using our life to bring hope to so many who had given up.

Since most of our traveling and speaking happened on the weekends, my weekdays were open to substitute teaching at

Parkview Baptist School where I had previously taught Bible. On one occasion, a senior student that I had taught the year before, told me the best news ever. She stated that she had watched me as I not only instructed students in the message of faith from God's Word but had also lived it. She was impressed with how I had drawn strength and peace and hope from God through trials and difficulties. As a result, she had received Christ as her Savior and Lord. That right there was enough for me to say, "it has been worth it all!" Clearly stated, our actions speak louder than our words. My favorite quote that hung in my classroom year after year was, "Your walk talks and your talk talks, but your walk talks louder than your talk talks." (Say that 3 times real fast!)

In order to help fund the Stroke of Love Ministries, I was afforded the privilege of recording a project to sell at venues where we spoke. This was a new experience for us as a family. The recording studio was located in nearby Prairieville, LA. It was owned and operated by a man who had been the bass player in a popular band in the 1960's. John Fred and the Playboys had recorded "Judy in Disguise". As we sang each song, we bore witness to these secular musicians of the greatness of our God. It was fun and very taxing. Jonathan and I were able to record, "Be Strong and Take Courage" which was the song he had sung to Robert in the emergency room. I also included "His Eye is On the Sparrow" in this project. As a Minister of Music, Robert had made many friends in the Christian music world. One such friend, Jack Price, who owned Prism Music produced 500 CDs and 500 cassette tapes for us at a very minimal cost. God provided.

In the year 1998, Justin and I experienced a mission trip to Russia with members from Temple Baptist Church in Hattiesburg, MS. Robert had served on staff at Temple prior to moving to Baton Rouge. We flew to Moscow and then traveled via bus to a camp for teenage orphans. There are so many orphans in Russia due to widespread alcoholism that renders parents as unfit to raise children. The main objective of this trip was to show these Russian teens how American teens trusted in God and lived according to

His word. Our host for the trip was the Deputy Prime Minister of Education for Russia. He was a Christian and wanted the youth of his country to see that there was a better way to live. This was a once in a lifetime experience for Justin and me. We were able to share of God's love not only with the teens, but also with the adult sponsors who were at the camp with them. They were so hungry for God's Word. We gave away Bibles that were written in the Russian language. I sang for group meetings and was able to give away CDs and cassettes to be distributed throughout Russia.

It did not take long for stroke survivors, with no local family, to begin to depend on me for transportation and minimal care. I was the one who was called when a fight with the now ex-husband caused a spike in blood pressure to the point of another stroke. I was the one who was called when transportation was needed to a meeting or healthcare appointment. Insurances didn't provide conveyance of patients in that period of time. Weekends were filled with trips to churches all over the South. I drove, I carried the luggage, I settled us into whatever the accommodations were provided, I pumped the gas, etc. I was the one who was substitute teaching during the weekdays. After three years of taking care of other stroke survivors as well as my own husband, speaking, and still raising a family, I was totally exhausted. God had a plan. He always does.

Most of our speaking engagements were booked by word of mouth. When we shared at a small church in south Louisiana, a survivor called her cousin, a pastor in northwest Arkansas, and insisted that he needed to have us speak at his church. Soon afterwards I received a phone call from Dr. Gibbie McMillan, pastor of Lakeside Baptist Church out from Rogers, AR, inviting us to share our testimony with his church family. Since Lakeside did not currently have a worship leader, Bro. Gibbie asked if I would lead the worship time in the morning service and then we would share our testimony during the evening service. I had never done that before but felt confident that having served alongside Robert for all these years and with his guidance, I should be able to do that for them. The entire weekend was such a wonderful experience. We were welcomed with such warmth and love. Shortly after our visit, the church asked us to move there so that I could serve as their worship leader. Our answer was "yes".

It was time for us to dissolve "A Stroke of Love" ministries and move on to what God had in store for our future. The excess funds in the ministry were surrendered to another Christian non-profit ministry lead by a dear friend named Cathy Arends. Cathy was a psychiatric nurse and perfect to reach out to those who were struggling with the new way of life that a stroke brings. She continued the support group meetings and caring for survivors. She was a single woman with far less demands on her life than I had.

"Well Done, My Child"

May of 1999 brought a host of great milestones in the life of the Goodman family. Aside from the Mother's Day holiday that rolls around every year, Robert and I celebrated 25 years of marriage (better than the national average) and our youngest son, Justin graduated from high school. There is so much satisfaction in seeing your children successfully cross over major hurdles in their lives.

It was during this time that Kathy Chapman-Sharp of LifeWay Press in Nashville, TN came to our home to interview the family. This was done for an article to be published in "Home Life" magazine. It was really a wonderful time of renewing an old friendship and discovering that the fifteen plus years had matured us all spiritually. (Okay, I can read your mind and I know that you are thinking about how much it changed us physically, too!)

It was during that interview that I began to discover things about my children that I did not know. Both Jonathan and Justin were willing to openly respond to questions that probed into their deepest feelings. This did not surprise me about Jonathan, but I was really shocked to hear Justin's feelings expressed openly. He has always been the quieter one of the two. I have to admit that when it comes to sharing our deepest thoughts, Justin and I are very much alike. We have learned to accept this because we realize that he is God's special design. Justin's words probably won't be quoted by great leaders for years to come, but I can assure you that there is a mother who will ponder them in her heart for a long time.

During his senior chapel at Parkview Baptist School, Justin sang the class song. That would seem like no great accomplishment coming from the Goodman family, but it was. You see, Jonathan had always enjoyed performing for others, while Justin would rather not be noticed. Justin's talents are great, but he would rather be a helper in the background. It took a lot for him to sing in front of 500+ students who are not always a user-friendly audience. Once again, his parents were very pleased and proud of his accomplishment and, for him, sacrifice. I was really glad that the video camera could not pick up the sound of tears flowing down my face.

"The father of a righteous child has great joy; a man who fathers a wise son rejoices in him. May your father and mother rejoice; may she who gave you birth be joyful!" Proverbs 23:24-25

When I think of that special bond that we as parents have with our children, I am reminded of an even more special bond that we as children have with our Heavenly Father. I think of how pleased I am with Justin, and I know that it can't even begin to compare with how God feels about me. I pray daily that I would never do anything to disappoint my Father. I know the pain I feel when one of my children makes a choice that I would not have chosen for them. I do not want to be guilty of making different choices from God's desire for me and thus hurting Him. Did you ever realize that you can hurt God? How it must break His heart to see how we treat each other and His world. I long for the day when I can hear my Father say to me, "Well done, my child," as He welcomes me into "the city that does not need the sun or the moon to shine on it, for the glory of God gives it light, and the Lamb is its lamp." Revelation 21:23.

All my good works and deeds on this earth are not what prompts God to welcome me into His kingdom. There is only one choice that will secure an eternity in His awesome presence. That choice is that I received the gift of salvation offered to me through God's Son, Jesus Christ. This gift is available to all who will choose to receive it. I think the simplest way to understand how is like A,B,C. A – admit to God that you are a sinner. B – believe that Jesus Christ is God's Son who gave His life to make atonement for our sins. C – Confess with your mouth that Jesus is Lord. You can pray to receive this gift anytime, anywhere. Here are some scriptures that might help you to understand.

A. Romans 3:23 – "For all have sinned and fall short of the glory of God"
B. John 3:16 – "For God so loved the world that He gave His one and only Son, that whoever believes in Him shall not perish but have eternal life."
C. Romans 10:9 – "If you declare with your mouth, 'Jesus is Lord,' and believe in your heart that God raised Him from the dead, you will be saved."

A PLACE OF HEALING
AND REST

-------- CHAPTER 8 --------

L akeside Baptist Church, doesn't that just sound peaceful? This church was nestled on the shore of beautiful Beaver Lake in the Arkansas Ozarks. It was located about 12 miles east of Rogers, AR on this 32,000-acre manmade lake. Lakeside was a small church with a big heart. We were excited to get back into the music ministry with such a loving congregation. With this excitement, also came sadness. We would be moving on but would be leaving our children behind. For the first time since their arrival into our lives, we would be separated from them by hundreds of miles. As a mother, this was hard, but we knew that we were serving God and that He would take care of all of us. We were now official empty nesters.

Remember that new house we built, we had to leave that too. Truly one of the hardest parts was leaving all our wonderful friends and supporters behind. These were the amazing people who had given sacrificially, not only financially but in so many other ways, to be sure that we had all that we needed. Parkview Baptist Church and School would now be a part of our history. It was extremely difficult for Robert to sit in the congregation and watch someone else lead the worship services that he had so dearly loved doing. As difficult as it was, we needed to move on.

Bro. Gibbie McMillan (Pastor of Lakeside) related to us how God led him to the place for us to rent until our house in Baton Rouge sold. The area around the church is called Beaver Shores and was really a very sought-after place to live. He told how he was driving around the area praying for God to provide a house. As he drove by a particular house, the homeowner was placing a sign in the yard that read "For Rent". He immediately stopped and inquired about the house. It was the perfect size, with the right price for temporary housing for us. The views of the lake were stunning. The church paid the rent for us until we were financially free from the Baton Rouge house. God never stopped providing and He never will.

I was still very busy unpacking boxes, when God used me to minister to a person that I have never met. Our phone repeatedly rang and when I would answer, the caller was expecting me to say "Walmart". You see Rogers is the home of the original Walmart. Its home offices were in Bentonville, the sister city of Rogers. I had to inform her that she had the wrong number. Again and again, it rang. Finally, the caller explained. Her husband who was a bi-vocational minister and also worked for Walmart had suffered a stroke. She was distraught and trying to reach the office for information and help with his medical insurance carried through his employment at Walmart. Wow! Could this be real? This lady was going through the same thing that I had gone through 4 years earlier. All unpacking ceased and I spent about an hour on the phone encouraging her, offering advice based on what I had learned, and praying with her. Only God could orchestrate such a divine encounter. As a footnote to this, my phone continued to ring with callers thinking they were calling Walmart. I finally called the home office myself to see if we could figure out what the problem was. The number I was given, when using the letters on the phone spelled out W-a-l-m-a-r-t, 925-6278. Employees could us a different area code and the letters to contact the office, but it had to be dialed from within a Walmart store. If they were not in a store, the calls came to me! I explained this to the phone company and they changed our number without charging us due to the circumstances.

My place for healing and rest was by a window in a small room of that house. This window had a perfect view of the sunrise over that lake. I met with God there every morning. He blessed me with spectacular scenes like you could never imagine. He is indeed a Masterful artist. No one can capture with paint or camera the beauty that I beheld each day. My faith grew enormously during this season of my life.

Our house in Baton Rouge soon sold and we started the process of building another home, this time on the side of a hill with a slight view of the lake in the winter when the trees were bare. Our builder was a deacon in the church and was very meticulous about each detail. I told Clyde (builder) that when we finished, I wanted the house to look 100 years old. It included stained glass windows, footed bathtub, antique mantle, pine plank pegged floors, punched tin kitchen cabinets and more! This was my dream home. For the first time in my life, the house included a basement. This was quite new to a Louisiana woman, because if you had a basement in Louisiana, it would just be an indoor swimming pool due to the extremely high water levels in that state. We finished out the basement with a living area, bedroom and bath just in case there was a need for us to be caregivers for my mom.

I loved the ministry at Lakeside. Even though the church was not large, we had an adult choir, student choir, and children's choirs. One of the members, Chris McCoy, loved drama so we regularly produced plays and invited the community free of charge. She also helped with Christmas drama and we even did a Living Lord's Supper. We did a series of weeks in which we focused on a certain era of hymn writers. Those who wanted, dressed in period clothing to celebrate the lives of our great composers. My friend, Cathy Dillard and I, sang a duet of "My Savior First of All" written by Fannie Crosby, dressed in Victorian attire! What fun and yet so enlightening into the lives of great Christians who lined the way for us today. I also was privileged to minister to the Senior Adult members of the church. You don't know what fun is until you've shared your life with these mature individuals. We made regular trips to Silver Dollar City in Branson, MO. We often went on outings to Kansas City, Kansas to the Titanic exhibit, Hallmark Building, and Arabia Steamboat Museum. We also went to Carthage, MO to the Precious Moments Chapel and Gardens. On multiple trips to Eureka Springs, AR we saw the Passion Play, other shows and went shopping. We journeyed to Oklahoma to the Will Rogers Museum. There was never a lack of something to do with these fun-loving seniors.

Not all fun was had at "work"! Saturdays in the summer were spent on the lake. Bro. Gibbie and his wife Katera owned a pontoon boat and a jet ski. We had also purchased a used jet ski. After the Saturday chores were completed, we would load up and head to the lake. Our ice chest was loaded with lunch, snacks and sodas. The rest of the day was spent swimming, riding jet skis, and jumping off cliffs. On occasion, our friends Joe and Cindy Curtis would bring their ski boat out and join us. When they did, we would water ski and be pulled behind their boat in an innertube type floatation device.

Winters were extremely different from anything I had ever experienced. It was not unusual to have several snow and ice storms. We made good use of those too. Bro. Gibbie would ride his four-wheeler over to the house pulling the hood of a car behind it. You've not had fun until you've ridden on that contraption in the snow! On one occasion, I walked to the mailbox and fell down seven times trying to return to the house. I finally crawled back. Jonathan and Justin were visiting during one of these storms and thoroughly enjoyed sliding down the hill on cardboard wardrobe boxes that we had used for moving. I do have to add that I didn't drive well on that stuff. I had two wrecks within three days. Not major, but due to the hilly conditions with few guardrails, it was frightening!

We often enjoyed visits from family and friends because we were located in such an excellent place for vacation fun. Our house was big enough to accommodate lots of guests at one time with four bedrooms and three baths. I loved entertaining guests both for extended stays and for a few hours. Once our abode was completed, we hosted an open house so that all the church members could see the finished product. I employed the cleaning lady from the church to help me keep it all clean. On one occasion, while Mary (cleaning lady) was there sprucing up, a friend of ours stopped by to see the house. Mary jokingly made the comment, "tell them the museum is closed for cleaning." We started an annual tradition of having a ladies' hat tea. I would polish the silver tea service and silver punch bowl, put out the finest linens I owned, made the canapes and put on my hat. These ladies had such a fun time. The variation in hats that were worn added to the gaiety of the event. They varied from baseball caps, to gardening hats, to Victorian chapeaus. Since we lived in a rural Arkansas area on the edge of the Ozark mountains, there wasn't much group social events like this for the ladies. We were never high class, just lots of fun!

It was not long before it became evident that I would need to serve as caregiver for my mom. An insurance salesman called me one day and began to explain that he had been at mom's house. He was very concerned because she had shown him her checkbook and all the personal information she had. He told me that he could have taken her for all the money she possessed, and that a less honest person would have. I had noticed that mom was having a difficult time communicating with me over the phone. I called her best friend and asked if she had noticed a change in mom. She confirmed that there was a problem. I concurred with my two brothers who lived close to mom, and we decided the best course of action would be for her to move into the living space in my basement. Around Thanksgiving in 2003, we moved some of her furniture and possessions to Rogers and set up her "home" with us. The first weekend after moving her, she became ill and was so winded that she was almost unable to ascend the stairs to the main level of the house. I immediately took her to the hospital. It was determined that she had congestive heart failure. The geriatric doctor ran tests and also confirmed that she had dementia. Though dementia and Alzheimer's are related in nature, the difference is the length of time from onset to death which sets them apart. With dementia, that time frame is about four years. With Alzheimer's, it could last up to twenty years. Decline is much more rapid with dementia. I have to state that were it not for an insurance salesman that I have never met, this story could have ended much worse. God was so good to give that man the wisdom to get my phone number from mom and give me a call. Once again, my God provided.

Things were changing at the church, as well. Bro. Gibbie had followed God's call to a position on staff in Texas. Our new pastor did not want women in leadership roles in the church. I told him that as soon as I could sell my house, I would move on. It didn't take long to sell the house. As a matter of fact, the real estate agent who helped me with the listing bought it. I need to tell you that soon after that family moved into the house, the husband/father was returning from a planning meeting where he was a worship leader, when he had a wreck on his motorcycle. He was wheelchair bound for quite some time. The house had been equipped for wheelchair accessibility when we built it, just in case Robert ever needed it. God once again provided not just for us, but also for this young family who, like our young family, had no idea that their life would be so drastically changed in the blink of an eye.

Our time in Rogers, AR was truly that place of retreat, rest and renewal, but now was the time for a return to life in a renewed way. There was still plenty of responsibility waiting for me as I returned to the place I had once called "home".

"The Four R's"

One of the most wonderful opportunities and responsibilities I have ever had was leading a group of ladies in worship at a retreat setting. It is so amazing how just a few short days away from our regular routine can change so much about us; our attitude, our energy level, our spiritual level and so much more. While reflecting on that retreat, I discovered the four R's that happen in our lives.

RETREAT – A change of scenery can be one of the most refreshing things we can do for ourselves. It doesn't have to be far. If you live in the city, the countryside is nice; conversely, if you live in the country, the city might be nice. Any change is good, if only briefly. In the book of Mark, we read about Jesus' teachings and feeding of the five thousand. Afterwards, He sent His disciples out in a boat, dismissed the crowd of people and in Mark 6:46 we read, "after leaving them, He went up on a mountainside to pray." We also learn from Mark's gospel, that once after an encounter with the Pharisees concerning clean and unclean foods, Jesus retreated to Tyre and Sidon. There He entered a house desiring that no one would know of His presence. Jesus, however, was a bit too popular to be hidden for long.

Find a place of retreat, if only for a few hours. Be alone with God. He has plenty to share with you.

REST – Immediately, most of us think of our Lord's words about rest in Matthew 11:28-30, "Come to me, all you who are weary and burdened, and I will give you rest. Take my yoke upon you and learn from me, for I am gentle and humble in heart, and you will find rest for your souls, for my yoke is easy and my burden is light." The writer of Hebrews encourages us in this same kind of rest in that we can give up on working to earn our salvation and come into God's rest. (Hebrews 4:8-11). Even our great and awesome God rested. Genesis 2:2 states, "By the seventh day God had finished the work He had been doing; so on the seventh day He rested from all His work." God sanctioned rest. He blessed rest.

Surely our spirit must come to rest in the arms of God and so should our bodies take some time off to rest from the usual routine of life. Imagine yourself as a small child curling up in your Father's lap and having Him put His loving arms around you as you drift off to sleep. Now that is rest!

RENEWAL – Definition: the replacing or repair of something that is worn out, run-down, or broken. With retreat and rest, we now have the opportunity in this precious time with our Lord to do some renewal on that child that has crawled up in God's lap. If you can imagine a complete renovation of your house: tear down walls, rip up carpet, yank out cabinets. What a mess! Now, pretend that everything new that was used to replace the old is sent straight from the Manufacturer. His work is so good that it is guaranteed for eternity. Do you think that you will be missing the old place? Below I have listed some scriptures that will help you to see what God's Word says about renewal. Delve into what He can do in you to make you a new creation.

RETURN – It certainly would be nice to remain on our retreat, but we must return to our world and share what we have learned. We must put into practice what God has taught us to do. We must care about the people who cross our paths on a daily basis. They need to know the Lord. God has called you to that responsibility. Romans 10:14-15 says, "How then shall they call on Him in whom they have not believed? And how shall they believe in Him of whom they have not heard? And how shall they hear without a preacher? And how shall they preach unless they are sent? As it is written: 'How beautiful are the feet of those who preach the gospel of peace, Who bring glad tidings of good things!'" We don't have to stand in a pulpit and preach the Word of God each week to be a preacher.

All we need to do is to live a life that glorifies God and by so doing give testimony to His goodness and love. People are hungry for what we have in Christ. They will ask. They want to know. We need to share.

Renewal Scriptures:
- Romans 12:2
- Titus 3:5
- Isaiah 40:31 (my favorite)
- Isaiah 57:10 (NIV)
- II Corinthians 4:16
- Psalm 51:10

HOMEWARD BOUND

— CHAPTER 9 —

Here we go again. This time it was literally "home" for me. We were moving back to Delhi into the house of my childhood. It was July, 2004, Robert had his gall bladder removed, our youngest son, Justin married the love of his life Jody, in Colorado and I was attempting to have mother's house in Louisiana renovated with the help of my younger brother, Bob. Add to that, I was once again packing up our possessions for yet another move. Not much going on! The kitchen of mom's home would be a total gut job with new cabinets and layout. Bob did the measuring; I went to the local home improvement store in Rogers to design and order the cabinets to be shipped to Louisiana. The plan was for the renovation to be complete by the time we got there with our possessions. Can I tell you that things rarely go as planned? For some unknown (to me) reason, the cabinets shipped through New Orleans. As they sat in limbo there, a "little" hurricane named Ivan came to town and flooded the warehouse, destroying my cabinets. We moved into the house with no kitchen. Imagine if you will, me taking care of a handicapped husband and a mom whose cognitive skills were diminishing, living in a house with no kitchen. To add to the scenario, the air conditioner died. We packed up the three of us and two cats and headed to a hotel. A precious friend of mom's insisted that we stay with her until the A/C was fixed at least. She was so dear to entertain mom while I worked at the house getting things unpacked. Once the air was fixed, we returned to the house without a kitchen. The pastor's wife loaned us a toaster oven in which to cook. I washed dishes in a plastic tub using the hot water from the garden hose which had laid in the sun in August in Louisiana. That is one of the most energy efficient hot water heaters you can ever use. "Roughing it" became a challenge that I soon embraced. Remember, if you can laugh at it you can live with it! My friend, Becky with her daughter Jourdan, came over and together we put together the pieces to make everything work. I had the stove delivered so that I could at least cook a decent meal.

It is now time for the second attempt at kitchen cabinets. I received notification that the truck would be delivering them. I anxiously awaited. Standing in the driveway. Hoping to flag down the driver. Being sure he found our house. Hours passed. No truck. No cabinets. Heartbroken at day's end, I went in to call someone, anyone to find out where my cabinets might be. I discovered that our land line phone was not working. Using my cell phone, I found out that the trucker couldn't find my house and when he tried to call, the phone was dead. He turned around and returned them to the warehouse! In researching the phone situation, we discovered that the plumber had severed the phone line in two places while working in the yard. I had asked him repeatedly to call the hotline to locate lines before he dug, but he had ignored my request. (This is where I would insert an angry emoji!) A few days later my cabinets were delivered and maybe you guessed…they were damaged! Oh well! Why was I not surprised? The contractor installed the good ones without countertops so that I could begin to do some type of normal cooking. Cardboard became the new look in countertops! By September, things were being finished up with just a few items that remained incomplete.

As we settled in, we returned to "normal" events. Church and choir were the mainstays of all of our lives. All three of us loved being a part of the choir at First Baptist Church of Delhi. That was "home" for us. It was where Robert and I met and married. It was where he served as Minister of Music during his college days. Old friends, new friends, people who loved us beyond measure were there for me. Help was only a phone call away. Mom was back to her familiar surroundings which is the best thing for someone with dementia. My brothers were both less than 40 miles away and ready to help out whenever I needed. I was able to get Mom into a class at the local hospital that helped her with using the skills that she still had. One of the greatest blessings at this time was my friend from the past named Tammy. She had just recently returned to Delhi as well and lived only a few miles from me. More than once, I had to call Tammy to come help me pick up Mom after a fall. She was always on call for me. I knew I could rely on her whenever I needed. I look back now and realize that God placed Tammy there for me "for such a time as this," Esther 4:14. God provided!

Mom's mental health continued to decline. Physically, she was still a strong woman, but lacked the cognitive skills to keep her going. She fell often, but never broke any bones which was a miracle. Her gaze always seemed to be off in a distance. Mom often called me "the momma" to Robert. I guess to her, it seemed that I was the momma taking care of the children, her and Robert. When you lose someone to dementia, you lose them long before their body gives out. I recall the horror of waking up one cold winter morning and finding that mom had fallen out of bed and spent the remainder of the night sleeping on the floor with no cover. She was so cold. I spend the next few nights sleeping in a recliner in her room so that I could be more attentive. I was able to secure a baby monitor which allowed me to return to my own bed for sleep. The days were long, and I was exhausted each night as I fell into my bed for rest. I have to be honest that I often questioned God about my life and how much more I could take. God knew how I felt. There was no need to attempt to hide that from Him.

Mom's doctor, Dr. Cory Albritton, was a wonderful Christian

man who attended the same church as us, sang in the choir, played in the praise band, taught Sunday School and so much more. He, too, was a God send. God Provides! Cory worked with me to help me care for Mom as long as was physically possible. When the time came, he helped me do the right things to make her transition to a nursing home go smoothly. We made sure that everyone understood that there would be no life support measures taken. On February 12, 2006, as I sat in church, my cell phone rang. I was mortified that I had forgotten to turn it off. I quickly switched it off, so as to not disturb others around me. After church, I listened to the message that Mom was declining rapidly and that I might want to come as soon as possible. That was the longest 20 mile drive I have ever made. I did get there before she slipped into the loving arms of our Savior. Peace! If you've ever loved someone with dementia, you know how mixed your emotions are. There is so little of who that person really was that still remains. You are so sad to lose them, but so glad that they are finally whole again. You lost their persona a long time ago. I have never regretted the opportunity I had to care for my Mom. I would do it all over again. We made some great, funny, forever memories during those years.

Dr. Marcus Murphy, pastor of FBC, Delhi preached her funeral. One thing that he always did at funerals was to research the meaning of the deceased's name. Mom's name, Marjorie, means "pearl". He expounded at length about how Mom was a rare beautiful pearl of great value to her family, her church and her community. The choir sang, since the choir and music was such a huge part of Mom's life. Yvonne Miers and her daughter Phyllis Pickett left the choir chair between them vacant because that was where Mom always sat. That tribute alone has been such a treasure in my heart for all these years.

Not long after Mom passed away, the worship leader at FBC resigned. I stepped in to lead the church in worship for the next few years. It was a joy to stand where my husband had once stood, leading choir and congregation to the throne of God. I was blessed beyond measure and God provided. "All good things must come to an end!" As the saying goes, that too ended, and I went to work as the human resources director for a local care agency for the developmentally disabled. My friend, Tammy, was the administrator of the facility. God provided me with a good job and health insurance. I learned so much from being around these precious clients and their caregivers. God opened my eyes to see and understand life from a totally different perspective.

Each morning on the local television station, at 7:30 a.m., the pastor of North Monroe Baptist Church did a 3-minute daily devotion. Robert and I made sure that we were tuned in each day to hear Dr. Bill Dye tell his awesome stories and then relate them to our walk with Christ. We decided that if that man could captivate us and touch our hearts in three minutes, we wanted to see what his full sermons were like. It took only one visit to North Monroe Baptist for us to know that we belonged there. It was a 45-minute drive one way, but so worth the time. We attended Sunday morning worship and "Lifegroup" (Sunday School) and Wednesday night choir rehearsals. It was this awesome body of believers that welcomed us and encouraged our walk. The "Rejoycers" class, as it was named after the teachers, Gary and Carolyn Joyce, were a servant-oriented class. They did so much to physically help us out. God provided!

After Mom's passing, my dad's cousin, Jeannette Reynolds, who lived about ¼ mile from us in the old family homestead became ill. Jeannette had never married. When she was just a small child, her father passed away. Her mom, along with Jeannette and her brother and sister moved back into the home place in order to survive. She and I shared a kindred spirit for sewing and embroidery. We also were members of the local service sorority, Beta Sigma Phi. I developed a bond with Jeannette even though she was 27 years older than me. Because of a lifetime of heavy smoking, Jeannette had developed nicotine poisoning that was destroying her kidneys. She had for years been struggling with breathing. More than once, she would call and I would go get her in the middle of the night and take her to the emergency room because she could not get enough oxygen in her lungs. As time progressed, she had to be prepped for dialysis. Once dialysis began, she moved in with one of her nieces in Monroe so that she could be closer for the treatments. One day she decided she didn't want to do this anymore. The doctor told her the alternative and she was ready. It was so difficult to stand by her hospital bed and watch her struggle with every breath. In March 2010, at the age of 82, Jeannette went home to be with the Lord. I never thought that I would be caregiver to yet another person, but God uses those who are willing to surrender to His calling. He provides the strength for each new day – one day at a time.

I began to assess our living situation and future needs for myself as I aged and for Robert whose health was always in the forefront of our lives. Looking around at the 51-year-old house with an acre yard, 4 bedrooms, 2 baths, 2 fireplaces, 2 septic tanks, 5 miles out in the country, I knew that it would be way too much for me to care for as I aged and continued to care for Robert. Though it was my childhood home and had been owned by no one but my family, it was time to sell the house and keep the memories. Even though we owned the house, I talked with my brothers about it and we all agreed that selling it and downsizing was the right thing to do. My widowed cousin, Lou, had recently built a small "garden" home north of Monroe. We attended an open house to see this perfectly sized home. We fell in love with the concept of less house and less yard. We began preparations to build our third house!

We chose the lot directly behind Lou's home, sold our house (which I always called Mom's house) promptly, without an agent, chose the same builder that constructed Lou's house, moved our belongings to storage and moved into the old home place left vacant after Jeannette's passing. Completing the house in August of 2010, that wonderful Lifegroup from church helped us gather all of our possessions from the various places we had stored them. "Downsizing" had become our life motto. In Rogers, our home was about 3,000 square feet. We "downsized" to 1,800 square feet to move into Mom's house which still had some furniture in it. Then from Mom's house, we "downsized" again to 1,200 square feet in our garden home. We successfully went from 4 bedrooms and 3 baths to 2 bedrooms and 2 baths. I have never regretted any of it. You learn just how much "things" and "stuff" can weigh you down. I learned that the more you have, the more you have to take care of. (Poor grammar I know, but great message.)

God's Word reminds us in Matthew 6:19-21, "Do not store up for yourselves treasure on earth, where moths and vermin destroy, and where thieves break in and steal. But store up for yourselves treasures in heaven, where moths and vermin do not destroy, and where thieves do not break in and steal. For where your treasure is, there your heart will be also." My God has always provided everything that we have ever NEEDED. The greatest struggles that we have as humans in the United States of America is differentiating between our wants and our needs. The media that infiltrates our homes on a daily basis is always telling us we NEED more. Friends, we don't. "And my God will meet all your needs according to the riches of His glory in Christ Jesus." Philippians 4:19. That is what this entire book is about, my God supplying all my needs. He is Jehovah Jireh, my Provider.

"Woe to Facebook"

Facebook. How many of us spend countless hours checking out what is happening in the world of our friends and family? It is indeed a great way to connect with those who live so far away. I love seeing pictures of my beautiful grandchildren who live 2 days away from me. My newsfeed is a powerful tool to ask prayer warriors everywhere to lift up special needs to our God and Savior. All said, Facebook can be a real blessing when properly used and monitored.

Lately, however, I've begun to focus on how good everything seems to be going for everyone else and not for me. Friends who started with us many years ago are renewing their vows on the beaches of Hawaii to celebrate their 40th wedding anniversary. My husband and I celebrated our 40th with dinner at the "Blue and White", a cinderblock restaurant in Lineville, AL. (Google maps will help you.) That same couple's grandchild lives in the same city as they do. Remember, mine are two days drive away!

Another friend that we made while in seminary so many years ago, has been to Disneyworld at least twice this year, if not three times. He even got to experience the Night of Joy Celebration with super concerts by today's best contemporary Christian artists. Poor Robert and I saved, scrimped and sacrificed just to spend 3 days there last year and couldn't possibly consider going back for another 5 years! By the way, they have 3 grandchildren who all live within an hour or two!

Woe is me! Poor me! Why can't life be easier for me? Why do I have to work 9 hours a day and barely pay the bills? Does that sound like the ultimate pity party? Yep, it sure is. I almost started crying on my drive to work, just thinking about all the unfairness of life. God knew my heart, heard my cry and saw my tears even before they were shed. In fact, He cares so much about me that He had already put His word in my "in-box" for me. That Word comes from 2 Corinthians 4:17-18, which says, "These hard times are small potatoes compared to the coming good times, the lavish celebration prepared for us. There's far more here than meets the eye. The things we see now are here today, gone tomorrow. But the things we can't see now will last forever." The Message. Amen and amen? It is not about what we have or don't have. It isn't about suffering or living on "Easy Street". It is about eternity! "No eye has seen, no ear has heard, no mind has conceived what God has prepared for those who love Him." 1 Corinthians 2:9 (NIV). All that gloriousness will last forever. What a wonderful hope we have in Him!

God reminded me that we spent our 40th anniversary with the best friends, that He created just for us. We have been so blessed in those 40 years and He has never failed us, nor will He. Our pastor did remind us in a sermon, that people don't typically put the bad stuff on Facebook, just the good. So remember that the next time you want to have a comparison pity party. A heart of gratitude for what we do have is the key to more than just surviving. We were made to thrive! "Those who sow with tears will reap with songs of joy. Those who go out weeping, carrying seed to sow, will return with songs of joy, carrying sheaves with them." Psalms 126:5-6

"WE ARE WITNESSES"

— CHAPTER 10 —

Recently, Robert and I had the wonderful privilege of singing in an Easter presentation at North Monroe Baptist Church entitled, "We are Witnesses". The musical reflected on so many New Testament people who had been direct witnesses to all that Jesus Christ had done as he walked on this earth during His three years of ministry, through His death and His resurrection. From His mother Mary, to the Samaritan woman, the twelve disciples, the Roman soldier who nailed Him to that cross and Mary Magdalene at the tomb. Each had seen first-hand what Jesus had accomplished in their own personal lives as well as in the lives of others. Woven throughout this drama was also testimony of modern-day people who had also experienced, seen with their own eyes what Jesus had accomplished in their own lives as well as in the lives of others. One of the keyboard musicians shared how God miraculously led physicians to find a fast-growing cancer and treat her to complete healing before the cancer had a chance to destroy her body. She was a witness to Jehovah Rapha's amazing healing. Another precious saint shared how she lost her husband and her son within a year, but God gave her strength and courage to face each new day. She was a witness to Jehovah Shammah's promise to never leave us or forsake us. Robert and I were thrilled to give testimony of how Jehovah Jireh has so abundantly provided physically, emotionally and spiritually more than we could ever need. The message is this: we didn't have to see Jesus on this earth with our own eyes in order to bear witness of what He has done in our lives. Every day we live as a witness to testify of His greatness in and through us. "Therefore, since we are surrounded by such a great cloud of witnesses, let us throw off everything that hinders and the sin that so easily entangles. And let us run with perseverance the race marked out of us, fixing our eyes on Jesus, the pioneer and perfector of faith." Hebrews 12:1-2a.

So where are we now? We are five hundred miles from that place I once called home in Delhi, LA. Five hundred miles from my brothers. Five hundred miles from where my parents are buried. Twelve hundred miles from our grandchildren and a mere four thousand miles from our oldest son. You get the picture. Cumming, GA is our new "home". However, God is still providing. Robert's awesome sister and brother-in-law have graciously opened their home to us so that I might not have to work up until noon on the day of my funeral. Their house has a two-bedroom apartment on the terrace level (we choose not to call it the basement) that has views of gorgeous landscaping, swimming pool, shade trees, and bird feeders filled with songbirds of all kinds as well as an occasional possum we named Pete. Trisha and Skip are never more than a few steps away whenever I am in need of help in caring for Robert. We have connected with a wonderful church called First Redeemer that has given us the opportunity to sing in choir and be a part of an amazing Connection group (known to most as Sunday School).

Just in case you are wondering, life has not been a piece of cake. There have been many, many struggles along the way, but God's presence in my life has given me the peace to handle each day, each trial, each move, each fall with the assurance that my God will supply all my needs. My prayer is that, as Paul wrote to Timothy, I may be able to say, "I have fought the good fight, I have finished the race, I have kept the faith. Now there is in store for me the crown of righteousness, which the Lord, the righteous Judge, will award to me on that day – and not only to me, but also to all who have longed for His appearing." 2 Timothy 4:7-8

The Wedding Banquet

During Robert's ministry at Parkview Baptist in Baton Rouge, he was privileged and honored to be a part of many weddings. Often, this also included an invitation to partake in the wedding feast that followed the ceremony. People in South Louisiana know how to put on a spread when celebrating a marriage. This particular one was held at the Camelot Club, an upscale, members only restaurant on the 26th floor of the Bank One Tower in Baton Rouge. The minister who had performed the ceremony and Robert who had supplied the music decided to stay together for security and company among many unknown guests. First on the agenda was to find the serving line and load up their plates from the delicacies offered for feasting. Next, they needed to find a place to sit in order to dine on their banquet. After looking around, they located several nicely dressed tables with linen tablecloths along the southwest side of the room overlooking downtown Baton Rouge and the mighty Mississippi River. They proceeded to take a place at one of the large tables with seating for 10 or more. It was only a few moments later, when the host informed them that they were sitting at tables reserved for the wedding party! Ouch! They politely removed themselves and found a place among the common people to finish their meal.

Such an incident at a wedding reception serves to remind us that there is coming a wedding feast, to which (as a child of God), I am invited and have a reserved seat. "Then the angel said to me, 'Write this: Blessed are those who are invited to the wedding supper of the Lamb!' And he added, 'these are the true words of God.'" Revelation 19:9. A lifetime of struggles will fade away into nothing compared to the joy that will be shared at that feast. Paul writes of his suffering in Romans 8:18, "I consider that our present sufferings are not worth comparing with the glory that will be revealed in us."

There is coming a day when Christ will return to gather His bride, the church, for the wedding feast in heaven. Will you be a part of the celebration? Will you be left behind? You can be sure that you will be a part by accepting salvation through Jesus' atonement for your sins.

BONUS DEVOTIONS

"For the Sake of Tradition!"

While Jesus walked this earth, He kept ever before Him, the need for people to be loved. The woman at the well – He showed love, compassion and forgiveness. The 10 lepers – He gave healing and comfort. The blind man – He restored his sight and his soul. Mary, who bathes His feet with her tears – He offered grace and honor. I could go on and on telling of the compassion Jesus showed to those who were so desperate for love, God's love, Agape love. This love reaches beyond what our finite minds can imagine.

Jesus loved so purely and unconditionally that it really disturbed Him to see the leaders of the church in Jerusalem doing everything but loving. In Matthew 15:1-9, Jesus reprimands these leaders, called Pharisees, for the way they hoarded finances and properties that are "devoted to God" and neglected the needs of their own fathers and mothers for the sake of tradition.

> "Then some Pharisees and teachers of the law came to Jesus from Jerusalem and asked, 'Why do your disciples break the tradition of the elders? They don't wash their hands before they eat!' Jesus replied, 'And why do you break the command of God for the sake of your tradition? For God said, "Honor your father and mother" and "Anyone who curses their father or mother is to be put to death."

But you say that if anyone declares that what might have been used to help their father or mother is 'devoted to God' they are not to 'honor their father or mother' with it. Thus, you nullify the word of God for the sake of your tradition. You hypocrites! Isaiah was right when he prophesied about you: "'these people honor me with their lips, but their hearts are far from me. They worship me in vain; their teachings are merely human rules.'"

Now let's fast forward a couple of thousand years to the church of today. Do we have a "woman at the well" who needs love and forgiveness? Today she might look more like a single mom. Do we have "lepers" who need healing and comfort? We might see them looking more like a homosexual in our world today. Do we know a "blind man" who needs his sight and his soul restored? Just maybe that man would look like a homeless person out on the street. What about a "Mary" who is pouring out her tears at the feet of Jesus needing grace and honor? Perhaps "Mary" is a fellow Christian who is struggling just to keep her head above water due to the uncontrollable circumstances in her life? Has God opened your eyes to see any of these people among you? Have you asked Him to let you see the hurting in your world? Just like the Pharisees of Jesus' time, we have leaders in our churches today who choose to follow "their teachings that are merely human rules" not only in the church's finances, but all other functions of the church "for the sake of tradition."

Is it now time to throw away the manmade rules, open God's Word and follow the leadership of our Lord and Savior in the way that we treat all human beings, whether they look like us, live on the same social status as we do, or even if they don't have the same sexual orientation as us? Now, I have shocked you! We will never win the lost and dead in sin to our Lord and Savior if we don't love all people in their sin so that we can lead them through the Spirit out of their sin and into the loving arms of Christ.

The Rose

An American tradition is that February 14th is Valentines Day. In my day, young school children made specially decorated boxes (usually from shoe boxes) to receive small cards from all their classmates. The day brings thoughts of love, chocolates and roses. Many a young (or older) lady would love to receive a dozen long-stemmed red roses on this special day. Such a gift would indicate love from someone very special.

Roses have a special place in my life for a different reason. I was named Rose after my grandmother. This has been a treasure to me since that grandmother died one month before my birth. It has been like a bond that ties me to the person that I never knew. I only know of the wonderful things that I have been told of her. I also like to grow roses. One Mother's Day, my family gave me four rose bushes. This is a very long-term way to give roses, but probably not romantic enough for Valentine's Day. I was able to enjoy beautiful, sweet smelling roses all summer long and well into the fall. For Christmas, Robert picked a theme for all the gifts he presented to me and you may have guessed, it was the rose. I received an original watercolor rose painting (done by him), a hand carved rose vase, with a fresh rose in it, a rose pin, rose stationery (using the original watercolor) and a swing to go under my running rose arbor.

Have you ever really thought about the rose? There are so many factors to consider when selecting roses. The first thing people usually consider would be the color. Red seems to be most desired, but maybe your personal preference is yellow or pink. Much depends on a special event in your life that might be remembered by the presence of a rose. Another describing feature of the rose would be the desired long stem. I guess this form is strictly one of functions, making it easier to arrange them when cut. The sweet aroma of a rose is yet a third consideration in selecting a rose. The first thing most people do when receiving roses is to smell them. What a wonderful sensation is the fragrant rose. Do you desire the roses to be fully open and mature, or choice buds that still have a lot of growing yet before them? No rose is complete without the thorns. We wish that they were not there, for these are the things that cause us pain when enjoying the beauty of the rose. Have you ever questioned why God did this? I have.

Now, I want you to consider your life as a precious rose that has been carefully and loving selected. You have made the choices. Did you choose Jesus? Is your spirit one of a sweet fragrance not only to God, but to those you meet in everyday events? How about your stem? Are you growing stronger in God's grace and mercy? Are you a maturing Christian, growing more beautiful with each day you spend in the Word? Now, what about those painful thorns? Are you breaking them off and giving them to Jesus or do you keep getting pricked by the same ones? "Brothers and sisters, I do not consider myself yet to have taken hold of it. But one thing I do: Forgetting what is behind and straining toward what is ahead, I press on toward the goal to win the prize for which God has called me heavenward in Christ Jesus." Philippians 3:13-14

You are so much more beautiful than the rose. You were created in the very image of God. Forget what is behind. Reach forward to what is ahead and become the most beautiful (spiritually) you that you can be!

The Driveway

January is typically a very wet month in our area. It is common for us to suffer flooded homes, out of work due to rain, new potholes or just plain gloomy attitudes. Isn't it amazing how 20-30 days without sunshine can really dampen your spirit? That is when we have to go looking for a ray of sunshine and inspiration in our lives.

I participated in a prayer group that met each morning and focused on that ray of sunshine and inspiration. God has shown us so many wonderful revelations about our lives and reminds us to keep our light shining even in a gloomy January. Our meeting place was at the end of a long driveway that had progressively gotten more holes and mud through the rainy month. God used even a "holy" (see what I did there?) driveway to reveal His encouragement to me.

When we first turn onto the driveway from the road, we cross over the largest hole of the entire path. This trench is an intentional one though and is covered by a cattle guard (or cattle gap, as I was raised to call it). This represents the really big devastations that cross our path. There is no way to go around them, but God has seen fit to provide a way over these chasms. Without Him, we simply could not proceed further.

Next, we come to a smaller hole that is really easy to go around. We can avoid some problems in our life by simply choosing carefully God's direction instead of our own. As we proceed, we come upon more of these smaller holes, but this time they are too numerous to go around them all. We find ourselves having to navigate through some in order to avoid others. There will be times along our path when we are going to have to actually go through some struggles, but God is still there to direct us and help us. When we get on the other side of these holes, we might even think, "That wasn't so hard after all!" Then we can easily praise Him for His direction.

There is still some rough road ahead. Now we encounter the really big, deep, ugly potholes. They are too big to go around, and you wonder if the car will make it through. Indeed, it does, but you can't help but be amazed. It is God who gets us beyond those great trenches in our life. This time He didn't choose to give us a cattle guard over it; we had to experience going through it. He never left us to go through it alone. He was there all the time. Can you still praise Him when He directs your path THROUGH the difficulties instead of around them or over them? Proverbs 2:8 says, "for He guards the course of the just and protects the way of His faithful ones." Aren't you glad that God does guard and protect us no matter what comes our way?

"I Am Adopted"

I know this will come as quite a shock to a lot of people, especially my mother, father and brothers, but I really am adopted. Don't get me wrong, I was born into a wonderful healthy family with a real mother and father who were never married to anyone else but each other. I have two terrific brothers, one older and one younger, who have always teased me (since I am the only girl and the middle child). I grew up on a farm with many grandparents, aunts, uncles and cousins close by. We attended church every week and my dad served as a deacon and Sunday School teacher. About the only "dysfunctional" thing about our family was that our mom worked outside the home when most of our friend's moms stayed at home. I think most of you would agree that if a working mom is the worst thing that happens to a family, then it must be a good home.

Now, about the adopted thing. You see, since our mom worked outside the home, she saw to it that we, the children, were raised properly. To do so, she hired a godly woman to stay with us in our home. Lena not only saw to it that we were physically cared for, but also many spiritual and moral lessons were taught. (She even made us go get the switch that she threatened to use on us and often quoted scripture to let us know just exactly what we had done wrong.) Lena and her husband, Claude, had never had a child of their own. Years later, I visited Lena in the nursing home. She very proudly told everyone who came into the room that I was her daughter. To some this would seem backed up by the fact that on her wall were the pictures of her mother, herself and me. Others would, however, have been taken back by the fact that Lena and her mother are African American, while I am about as lily white a Caucasian as God ever made. This fact didn't seem to bother either Lena or me. I am her daughter.

Scripture tells me of another adoption. This adoption I share with my real mom and my adopted mom. "For He chose us in Him before the creation of the world to be holy and blameless in His sight. In love, He predestined us to be adopted as His sons (and daughters) through Jesus Christ, in accordance with His pleasure and will." Ephesians 1:4-5. Now, the way I see it, this adoption makes the three of us sisters in Christ and joint heirs with Jesus. (Do you think anyone will notice that our brother is a Jew? I'm so glad that God is color blind.) Because of this adoption, our inheritance is out of this world. "Now if we are children, then we are heirs – heirs of God and co-heirs with Christ, if indeed we share in His sufferings in order that we may also share in His glory." Romans 8:17. If you have not yet been adopted by our Heavenly Father, It is not too late. He is waiting with His arms open wide, ready to receive you as His child.

The One True Light

Recently I was given the gift of a blue star sapphire ring. The blue stone looks much like just an ordinary polished rock that has a dark blue color. Not real impressive at first glance. You would notice the stone's mounting and other elements of the ring before you would complement the stone itself. Inside a building, the light would cause other stones, such as the diamonds mounted around the rock, to sparkle and glimmer with extraordinary beauty, but not that blue rock. Inside, there are many sources of light, and many kinds of lights. However, if you step out into the sun, the true beauty of this rock appears. As the sun, which is the only source of light outside, shines on the stone, a beautiful white 6 faceted star radiates inside the rock. As the ring is moved to reflect the sun's light, so does the star move around inside the stone. That star follows the direction of the sun, moving always to face the source of light. It is fascinating to watch as this amazing creation can change from responding to many lights indoors and the one light of the sun.

Such is the life of humans. We have hidden inside each of us the potential for a radiantly beautiful star shining forth from our souls. This beauty is diminished and hidden when we surround ourselves with the world. Enclosed and dark is our lives when we live for this world. Romans 12:2 reminds us," Do not conform to the pattern of this world but be transformed by the renewing of your mind." It is only when we step outside of the world into the Son, Jesus Christ, that the true beauty of our souls radiates like a shining star as His creation. In John 8:12, Jesus speaking to a crowd of people said, "I am the light of the world. Whoever follows me will never walk in darkness but will have the light of life." He is the only Light that can make our lives shine. Jesus Himself told us in Matthew 5:14-15, "You are the light of the world. A town built on a hill cannot be hidden. Neither do people light a lamp and put it under a bowl. Instead, they put it on its stand, and it gives light to everyone in the house. In the same way, let your light shine before others, that they may see your good deeds and glorify your Father in heaven." Just as the star in the ring moves around in the sunlight, we reflect the beauty of His light as we live and breathe and have our being. The key to reflecting His beauty is to always be turned in the direction that faces Him. Turn toward the source of light. How do we do that? He has written an entire book that guides us and teaches us about Himself so that we may know Him and strive to be the creation He designed each one of us to be. Search His Word. Spend time in prayer. Meditate on His Word. Fellowship and study with other believers. Seek counsel from people of God. You too can be a beautiful reflection of His amazing Light in you!

Celebrate

Celebrate! The very word itself calls for rejoicing. When I looked in my NIV Bible Concordance for the word, I found fifty-three references that used the word "celebrate". Forty-seven of those fifty-three are in the Old Testament and are referring to commands that God gave His people to worship and obey Him through some type of celebration. Think about these times of rejoicing:

Passover – Remembering the last plague in Egypt, when the angel of death "passed over" the children of Israel who applied the blood of the lamb to their doors. This lamb's blood saved the Israelite firstborns, but Jesus became the lamb Who came to save all who believe on Him. (Leviticus 23:4-8)

Feast of Unleavened Bread – A seven-day feast on the day following Passover. In their haste to leave Egypt, there was not time to wait for bread to rise from the yeast (leaven) added to their bread. During this time, the Jews were to remember the hardships in Egypt and how God delivered them from captivity. Jesus later states that He is the bread of life. He removes our sins and nourishes our souls. (Leviticus 23:6)

First Fruits – One of three harvest feasts to thank and honor God for all He provided. Little did the children of Israel know that they were celebrating what would eventually be the day of resurrection of our Savior, Jesus Christ. (Leviticus 23:10)

Feast of Weeks or Pentecost – The second of the three harvest feasts. It occurs seven weeks after the Feast of First Fruits and is called Pentecost which means "50 days". It was on the day of Pentecost that Jesus' disciples gathered in one place received the Holy Spirit and became bold witnesses of Jesus. (Leviticus 23:16)

Feast of Trumpets – A time of rest. During this time, all regular work is prohibited, men and women present a food offering to God. It is to be commemorated with trumpet blasts. The trumpet blast is associated with the rapture, or the time when Jesus will return for His bride, the church. (Leviticus 23:24)

Day of Atonement – This day was designated as the day that the High Priest would enter the Holy of Holies in order to make atonement or payment for the sins of the people. The sacrificed animals were an offering of thanks, but the "scapegoat" (Leviticus 16:10) took on the burden of their sins and was sent out into the wilderness. Praise God, Jesus' death on the cross eliminated our need for further atonement. (Leviticus 16, 23:26-32)

Feast of Tabernacles or Booths – This is a seven day celebration beginning on the day after the Day of Atonement. It is designed to celebrate God's provision during the 40 years of wandering in the wilderness. During these days, people live in temporary structures like they did in the desert. God Himself dwelled among them in a tent called the tabernacle. His presence, His dwelling is celebrated. Today, Jesus is called Emmanuel which means, "God with us". His Spirit dwells in our hearts and lives. As Christians, our bodies are His temple. (Leviticus 23:34)

How much more do we have to celebrate today? The Old Testament believer had to work to earn their eternal salvation and all we must do is accept the free gift of life through Jesus Christ our Savior. Yet do we celebrate? Do we rejoice in worship? Have we lost the joy of our salvation? I love the song, "Celebrate, Jesus, Celebrate". It is so full of happiness that God intended for us to share with Him. Take time to celebrate all the great things that God has done for you. Tell Him. He loves to hear His people praise Him.

Mt. Pinatubo

(written by Robert Goodman prior to his stroke)

In 1991, Mt. Pinatubo in the Philippines erupted with such power that the largest plume of smoke measured 15 miles in the air. Ash, rocks and volcanic material were showered as far away as 20 miles. The resultant cloud affected weather and airline flights as well as the general health of livestock and humans.

Short of the atomic bomb, only Mount Saint Helens exhibited this kind of destructive power. As I reflect on the havoc created by these explosions of nature, I realize that we know the One Who has such power. Yet His love for us through Jesus stays His destructive power towards us and gives us life eternal.

We are bestowed with a power that is beyond our imagination. The apostle Paul's prayer was to know Jesus in the power of His resurrection. That was the power of God to raise Jesus from the dead. When Jesus gave the great commission, He said, "All power has been given unto me in heaven and on earth." You see, we have that power too, because Jesus is in us.

Ephesians 6:10 says, "Be strong in the Lord and in the strength of His might." We are His witnesses, clothed in His armor, and we have power in the spiritual realm, power in the Name of Jesus, the only name given unto men whereby they can be saved.

So, remember, we have a witness to share and the power and strength to share it. Jesus said He would never leave us or forsake us.

When we really realize the power of God to create a universe, to give us life and to give us new life in Christ, we should stand firm in our faith – built on the foundation of Jesus and know that we can do all things through Christ, who gives us strength. It is His power in us. May we covenant together to be God's powerhouse – to share the gospel of light with a dark and lost world.

Dig Deeper: Think of the times you may have failed or didn't do your best. Was it because you were working in your own flesh? Let us labor in the strength of God.

Scripture:
- Psalm 28:7
- Isaiah 40:29
- 1 Peter 4:11
- 2 Corinthians 12:9

It's A Wonderful Life

(Written by Robert Goodman prior to his stroke)

Have you ever wondered what life would be like if you weren't here? Or what would life have been like if you never moved to where you live now – or if you moved away? All of us experience days when we'd love to be somebody or somewhere else. However, God has us right where He needs us!

An annual tradition in the Goodman household has been and continues to be, watching the great classic movie, *It's A Wonderful Life*. In short, George is contemplating taking his life because of bad circumstances in his job. His guardian angel, Clarence, comes to his rescue. When George wishes he had never been born, Clarence shows him exactly what the world would have been like if he had never lived. At one point in the movie, Clarence states to George, "You've been given a great gift, George, a chance to see what the world would be like without you." Another time he said, "Strange, isn't it? Each man's life touches so many other lives. And when he isn't around, he leaves an awful hole, doesn't he?"

In all my years of ministry, I've had several calls from churches needing a new worship leader. Some were real inviting – others, not worth the time – or so I thought. Once, a large church in the Southeast got in contact with me. Within four days, my wife and I had emotionally moved – and yet God really never opened a door to move. I was trying so hard to move, but God had me right where I was supposed to serve.

There are days when everyone feels worthless and out of place. Mainly because pride gets in the way. We feel that no one notices our abilities and talents, or we aren't getting appropriate attention. God tells us to be still and know He is God.

It's when we get our eyes off Jesus and on ourselves that the balance of life goes haywire. We think we're unimportant; we're not talented because we didn't get chosen for a promotion or special task. We feel we've been forgotten. However, God promises He'll never leave us or forsake us. He has us in a certain place to minister to a hurting individual or group of folks. The Psalm writer tells us that we are fearfully and wonderfully made. God knows our potential and is working to make us all that He knows we can be.

Stay close to God. Allow His voice to minister to you. He is saying, "You are valuable to me. I have plans for your life." Don't wish it away or desire to move because you're unhappy with your circumstances. God wants you to depend on Him and allow Him to use you as a minister – right where you are.

You may be feeling like a forgotten person but believe me and the Word of God. It's a wonderful life, and God wants to do great things through you. Just open up to His leadership. Make an effort to minister to someone today. Find, understand and comprehend your self-worth in God.

Dig Deeper:
➲ Psalm 139:13-14
➲ Proverbs 3:5-6
➲ Philippians 1:6

Friendly Fire

(written by Robert Goodman prior to his stroke)

During the early 1990's the U.S. was engaged in a conflict in the Middle East called Desert Storm. It was paramount in the minds of so many who had loved ones involved in fighting in this war. All kinds of stories have surfaced from this conflict. Stories that teach us. Mistakes that mark us but help us to learn and seek God more.

"Time Magazine", February 18, 1991, records that Iraqi tanks perched on the north side of a sand ridge near the Saudi-Kuwait border were firing at a company of U.S. Marines on the south side. The Marines were returning fire with TOW antitank guided missiles. Overhead, a U.S. Air Force A-10 Thunderbolt swooped toward one of the Iraqi tanks and released a heat-seeking Maverick that smacked into the left side of an American light armored vehicle, blowing up the vehicle and killing all seven Marines inside.

The tragic exchange was one of the first engagements of the ground war and opening rally in the 36-hour battle of Khafji. It also represents this war's first documented case of U.S. casualties from "friendly fire" – a combat euphemism for troops getting shot, shelled or bombed by their own side.

How many times have we been guilty of "friendly fire"? Many times, as Christians, young and old, we have a tendency to get in a "dig" or make a critical comment toward another person. This can be devastating to a fellow Christian who is struggling with their own spiritual identity and growth, not to mention self-esteem. Think also how horrible this is to the non-Christian who is looking to us for something different from what the world has to offer.

What kind of effect does this have on those whom we call "friend"? Around our home, we strive to always make building statements, words that encourage or build up the other. I'll admit, there are times when I'm guilty of "friendly fire". I'm not proud of it either. Let's lay our weapons (words) down and learn to be encouragers. We all need a more peaceful sense of self-esteem. In a world of monumental depression, let's be bearers of good tidings, and build up one another. As Thumper's dad told him in the Disney movie *Bambi* "If you can't say something nice, don't say nothin' at all."

Dig Deeper: Is there someone I need to ask forgiveness for "friendly fire"? Look for a way today to encourage someone.

Read:
- ➲ Ephesians 4:29, 31-32
- ➲ Philippians 2:3-4
- ➲ I Thessalonians 5:11,15

Printed in the United States
by Baker & Taylor Publisher Services